Down by the Eno,

Down by the Haw

The word I think of with this stunning almanac is *range*. Moeckel ranges far and deep, farther and deeper than he has ever gone, while mostly "sitting and looking around" the Piedmont of North Carolina. And this wondrous epic expands his range as a poet, the language in these prose poems facile, playful, breathtaking. The sure-footed Moeckel torques poetry out of wandering in place, with breath itself a dance and an exploration. "There are roots in my lungs," he writes. And "I turtle on a fallen pine." One of my favorite poets has outdone himself. This book is delicious, inspiring, impressive.

—Janisse Ray, author of
Ecology of a Cracker Childhood
and *The Seed Underground*

Down by the Eno, Down by the Haw is so rhythmic and rhymed, so riddled with light and webbed with spidery strands of connection, it moves the mind right past the obvious praise—that this prose sounds like poetry—to a stance of truer wonder. Moeckel is not the kind to let us be distracted by categorization, remarking about a bird, "If I knew its name, I wouldn't say it. If I didn't know its name, I'd make one up." His humility is earnest as his lyricism is grand, and Moeckel *does* intimately know the inhabitants of Piedmont environment to which he has committed himself, observing the compromised landscape with an awareness so enamored of every detail it is also "promiscuous." In the moments you are able to spend with these pages, you too will be let in on the beauties tucked into the woods behind shopping plazas, and to a way of thinking and seeing that can, with what is gathered in some short lunch break walking, make the troubled-of-heart believe again that this world's tangles are where we are blessed to be ensnared.

—Rose McLarney, author of
Forage and *Its Day Being Gone*

I was born in the North Carolina Piedmont and have lived for the last year within sight of the Haw River, but Thorpe Moeckel's *Down by the Eno, Down by the Haw* has gloriously revealed my ignorance of the region. This is fitting, since the book is a meditation on not-knowing, belied by Moeckel's exhilarating knowledge of the names of things, of the cadence of consciousness, of ways to hear and methods to see beyond, beneath, above. Moeckel observes and records with the humility of a man who knows that every moment is tenuous, every vista shifting. "I like words," Moeckel writes, "but I like woods better." That he finds the words to bring these woods to such wondrous, vibrant life is what makes this book so necessary. I've not read a book in years that bears witness to beauty with such selfless and artful gratitude.

—Michael Parker, author of
Everything, Then and Since

MERCER UNIVERSITY PRESS

Endowed by

TOM WATSON BROWN
and
THE WATSON-BROWN FOUNDATION, INC.

Down by the Eno,

Down by the Haw

A WONDER ALMANAC

Thorpe Moeckel

MERCER UNIVERSITY PRESS

Macon, Georgia

1979–2019

40 Years of Publishing Excellence

MUP/ P590

© 2019 by Mercer University Press
Published by Mercer University Press
1501 Mercer University Drive
Macon, Georgia 31207
All rights reserved

9 8 7 6 5 4 3 2 1

Books published by Mercer University Press are printed on acid-free paper that meets the requirements of the American National Standard for Information Sciences—Permanence of Paper for Printed Library Materials.

Printed and bound in the United States.
This book is set in Adobe Caslon Pro.
Cover design by Burt&Burt.
Catalpa image by Josef Beery (www.josefbeery.com)

ISBN   978-0-88146-721-5
Cataloging-in-Publication Data is available from the Library of Congress

CONTENTS

for Mom

Down by the Eno,

Down by the Haw

ONE: (UN)BECOMING

February
Wet (Mud Month)

They go on *as running water, in and in*, the days, nights, borders. February's februations. These jaunts, these woods. I need this. On the way to the grocery. Behind the job at lunchbreak. Tangly places, little creeks, roots, stumps. Groves and glades. Copses. I try to get lost, try to see. See, edgewise, these edgeplaces, and on, into—if lucky—the beyond, the here in it. On the way to the lumber store, I cross the bridge. Slow down, pull off, find a way in. There's time, the river, slatish olive and pungent. Boils bloom, brief mandalas, off the bluff where I stand, icy snow bouncing off my jacket.

Pulpy aromas fill me with many rivers and winters and walks. Lost by finding. In being found, a losing, a slough. Many lives (some of them my own?). I need this. If compulsion, if communion. Something. The edge's centers or how the edge is centered. A sycamore juts off the bank at the waterline, yesterday's snow a frayed sock on its upstream edge. It does nothing, this sycamore, does everything; a dogwood log, remnant of higher water, leans across its trunk.

What appears to be a shoe, an old boot drifting past, turns out on closer inspection to be a bottle, an old one still capped. Something. Another if or or. I walk some more.

Sleet gathers in the grass, comes to rest on the leaves of the mustard greens. The air tastes like joy, like screaming, screaming with joy, joystreams. Snow mixes with the sleet. Already the day feels less busy than it did twenty minutes ago, and yet it feels more urgent, more empty, more alive.

Small birds call more than sing. I keep thinking a thing's alive under the water every time it boils, that a muskrat, beaver, or fish has nearly surfaced. But then I see that it's release, release of energy, water flowing in another direction. And then another.

The snow's heavy, the flakes conglomerations of many flakes, and the driest seat's a root curling out and then into the bank. I face upstream and across. Submerged rocks, moss-soft, the size of deer skulls, wrinkle the water, lending topography to the sky and trees reflected there. The snow vasty over the land. Skins, a skein of skins. I try to be still so the birds will return. When I turn my head, I do so slowly. My eyes move slowly, too, and with as little threat as I can breathe for. But it's difficult not to whip my amazed face around when the woodpecker does its gravity dance three feet from my head. Snow sloughs from branches as the checkerback knocks a maple's limb. Below, a wave—water pressed between stones—trickles at a tempo so regular it catches my ear long before I know it.

Easy as pulling over, putting it in Park. In the Piedmont, there are woods, densities (changing) behind most every boxstore, strip mall, church, school. Creeks where I least expect them. Few vistas mean more surprises, more searching. I walk. I sit. I walk, stand, shed a little skin.

But what a ruckus, the beaver pond yesterday. Everywhere there were birds, heron, geese, woodpecker, also songbirds small, small and quick. I sat at the edge of the rushes. Spiky clumps of tan and green gave way to Japan grass and ground scattered with deadfall, broomsedge, the scarecrowish young loblollies. My eyes drifted like the birds across the pond, to that maple, that pine, and then back again.

Maybe flight's easiest. Maybe it's landing that needs practice. Or is it that landing means being okay with flight? Or is it less flight, less landing than being, simple as that? *A bee, angling.* Something. A tangled something. Tangled briars, some laden with a few desiccated grapes. I noticed barbed wire, rusty, a kind of petrified briar, rising from the mud towards a lichen- and moss-limned cedar post. This was yesterday. This was morning. The days, gracious, they can feel ancient, fused with the land.

Especially the warm, February days before the trees have any leaves and most of the flowers are but a promise. Only the water and the trees seem still now, but even stillness is illusion, illusion another word for hope.

I hope to see. I hope to be surprised, split open from the eyes down to the heart, reaches of arteries, reaches of veins. Marrow, too. Somewhere and somewhere else and so on. A kind of lust. Hunger, at least. For living, for life. What else is there? Need it is, a need and a hope that these woods might blind me to sight.

It slides on, February, cunning month: as fast as it tickles, it retreats, grows harsh and inhospitable enough to be promising yet. Can be gaunt and snappy and grey as an old branch, February, or moist and squishy as a bog's perimeter. Can be meatier than sap or aired and gleamy as a fingernail moon.

Nothing's still. I'm looking at a fallen pine tree and hearing a deer, maybe more than one, move through the leaves. The skymilk. The pine branches, scimitars. Yellow-brown bundles of needles hang from branch-ends. A paler yellow, the Japan grass, than last month, flaxier, mulled as if with orange essence (the nose says cloves, too). It's dead, the Japan grass, winter dead and wilted, yet it drapes over the fallen pine as if placed there, and I love it. I love it all, how the deer pellets, late berries, litter the sweetgum nut husk- and pinecone-littered Japan grass at my feet. How, as far as I can see, which isn't more than twenty yards before the land slopes, Japan grass lies over the ground like a blanket. How it's layered, too, the grass, with pine needles. How over the fallen pine it bends, the Japan grass, and over the stumps and branches.

The pond is bank-full again. A light breeze carves peninsulas of bright on the eastern flank. Then it's gone, the wind, and the sky is a loaf, doughy and darkly lit. I can't tell whether a front's moving in or out. The alders, maybe, speak of it. The quiet, as usual, makes its racket. Needles flutter. Branches creak and rub.

On a fallen limb, pinecones, little bulges. Even the bark, cinnabar and deeply grooved, whispers in chilly silences sweet everythings and other nonsense.

Rain begins. I see its saucers on the pond before I hear or feel it. It is rain, it is gentleness. Isn't it. Now geese arrive, their voices at least. *By throat, by rinse, by yearn, scrim, glide, by glow.* When the world is like this, I know what to do. I sit. The world is always like this, and I don't always sit but go ahead, man, you've got a little time—set your fanny down, and look, and don't look, and see what you see.

Here are feathers, small ones the grey and blue of a titmouse. They litter the peak of a fallen branch not four feet away. How far that closeness was until now, and farther still even inside. Must be a common feeding place for some critter, that branch, as the husks of hickory nuts fill grooves in bark and splintered timber. I sense a squirrel hunched and munching, and then that image superimposes on an owl disemboweling a songbird, a muskrat following up to gather the scraps. I feel it. And I feed.

6

This poking around, this looking and walking, sitting and trying to see. None of this will make the news. Feathers are not newsworthy, nor geese nor pinecones, especially not the quiet of the sun and the breeze smooching the pond's face.

To know the seasons as the trees; to fail to understand what the breeze knows, but to try; to wonder the woods, the changes, to sense them, to feel them as moles know stones through the quality of the soil; to touch and suck; to taste, touch, flail; to be mineral, to be shrub and grub and shadows of shrubs; to know the sound of running water as if salamander, toad—this is the news I need.

Warmth arrives, and the snow weeps with it. Delirious warmth. I'm giddy. I could hardly wait for lunch, and now it's here, and I've slipped into the floodplain beyond the parking lot at work. Sun on the river smells chalky and alive. The air or the light or the maze of growth leads me to a sandy steppe below a bluff's crest. More softness here, stone crushed nearly to soil, soil, leaf debris and silt. In the shade of stumps and roots, snow persists, swaths as if old tissue. I'm giddy with the promise of blossoms, buds. There's sap in us, and I want to know its rise.

A woodpecker lands, squeaks as it takes off again. Hinges: a streak of broomsedge, a sycamore, a finger of blue in the river's sulfur. *Ganglia, gumshoe, presence*—words ooze as if laughter, the giggles of an excited mind.

I swim in the day's many rivers. Wind eddies behind the shadow's song. Birdchirp shines. The land walks under the deer. Even the noise is quiet, though the quiet makes a pattern, a leafy one and veined.

The floodplain woods always suck me farther than I intend at first to go. I curl between river maple, beech, hackberry, sycamore. Other trees, too, both rotting and alive—hornbeam, cedar, poplar, oak. Limbs and branches tangle with vines and light, and old leaves lure me, wiggling dorsal and relaxed into a river of

7

wonder. Two titmice call and respond from opposite banks, four high-pitched squeaks, nearly squawks. The rusty hinges of chickadee voices are ceaseless like the gurgle of a riffle downstream.

The river's swollen still from Friday's rain and the snow that it melted. It's silted and hashed with stretchmarks of light where the breeze—not quite warm, not quite cold—ruffles it. I feel an urge to jump in, but then all water has that effect. A shard of once clear plastic hangs in a sycamore that grows, lizardly and split-trunked, over the river at a rough forty-five. If I had a crayon, I'd try to draw the tree, the plastic, the river. By never getting it right, I'd get it rough, right.

There's a place in these woods, a seepy place, and it pulls. Look, nobody needs anything from me here. Nobody's telling me to do more, make more, have more. Running deer define the farthest point of vision—even then. The duff's soft, damp, and steamy with morning sun. Crows ruckus in the pines to the west; maybe they're harassing a hawk.

When I meet a path, I cross it and keep walking until I find the place, a poplar's sloped trunk. Gashes in the ground mark springs, seepages, small bogs. I love the beech leaves airing out, dainty, more brittle in appearance than in actual life. Tiny geysers of mist broil off the pinebark, the east-facing scales. In my legs, odd nerves flutter as though little critters are trying to crawl out and enjoy these woods without me.

Sphagnum hillocks border the seeps' edges. Sphagnum, fringed with the hair-like growth of gymnosperms. Some seeps seep small, the size of puddles; others extend to a diameter of twenty feet across, and being seeps (seepish) and true, they're far from perfect circles.

Who knows what brought me here this morning, what impulse or seed, but by breathing, sometimes softly, I try to thank it. What else can I do.

I'm done, and the days go on, doing me. Once more, I've followed deer tracks to a place in the woods. Once more, the weather has changed. Dry snow clings to limb, trunk, branch, two inches of the light, small flakes on the ground. Wind arrives, clearing the limbs with sudden showers cold on the neck and face. Cedars lean with the white weight. Everything seems enlarged, both itself and a bust of itself. Shadows are a pale violet and they travel more loudly. I sense a false urgency about the day. It's quieter than ever yet dares to be beholden, now sultry, now coy.

The canopy is changed. All the limbs hold the light and the dark differently. They stand in a changed relation to one another. Changed is not always charged, but they're mighty close today. If I was a bird, say a chickadee, I'd want to be careful to adjust my flight pattern. As it is, I'm a person with a little time and a decent pair of rubber boots.

Light so wrought I can't think. Seems I'm breathing iron as I trudge the ridge beside the creek. Seems, well, it seams. A white oak becomes my backrest. Beside me a birch elegantly splotched, and next to it an old cedar, polished, knobby, sensual with holes and sinuous grain on growths. If the woods of the Piedmont are clumsy and knock-kneed, there is grace nonetheless (that of a merciful, polite crowd).

As it is, I'm a person who on many days, until I get in the woods, feels very far from myself. The woods right me, as it is, they whole me, if for a while, and soul me. The Piedmont woods—settled for so long, compromised, torn up (*worked*) and enduring as they are—tender me. They swale, they bail me.

9

As it is, I don't trust it, fret what's good for me. Is it good then? What do I deserve? It's not that I don't live a regular, decent life. I have many things. I eat well. My clothes are presentable. I have the necessary comforts and the unnecessary comforts. Such having, I have it.

The days, the life within and around me, I try to open to it every way I can. I try to say yes to everything, even when I say no, I say yes, yes, sorry, I say sorry, and I say sorry, yes, let me change that, fix this. I say yes perhaps too much. I say yes perhaps to bad end, as if the yes, no matter how it sounds, looks like no.

Even in the woods, as they are, I'm nothing, and I like it so much I hardly allow myself to like it, and this is okay, this is not unusual, but I don't know that yet, might never know that.

February, it's a ghost, and I track it as best I can. I want to be captured more than to capture, by some essence of this place. How foolish, and yet. And where is not of the essence, but what, and how that what, and less the why of it. I stare at the lines of a moss-quilted boulder. The colors harmonize with innocent abandon. It feels as though every leaf has a heart but not a beat, and then as if there's a pulse without any organ at all. But wind and weather and gravity, they sail along the same quotient: *decay, rebirth, decay, rebirth.*

Nothing changes, and everything, and I feel, as ever, as captive as released. In the duff, an old blackberry hardened by the equivocating winter appears upon closer inspection to be an acorn cap. I like being wrong. How else does learning speak? We are born wholly and as we age grow holy. The land reminds me of my prodigal essence and also hints that being prodigal isn't necessarily immoral, that it just hurts sometimes.

10

And the stinkbug crawling up my sleeve I take as a stinkbug and not a sign to stop.

All these browns and caramel colors of February, the barks' greys and rusts, they're glazed as though from within, with a blue the odor of coming to the surface after a long time under.

I've never gone to the woods to fashion a palette for myself, but it helps. It helps me respond to the lands I've loved and left—the mountains, the desert, the sea—and the people of those lands with whom I've shared in love and fumbling.

Here's the sun, you see, blowing a luminous pollen over everything, the wood, the air, the water, the stone, and their derivatives: soil, chlorophyll, flesh.

If I'm lucky, I'm continuing a conversation already continued by any being with a hunger or even by the simplest cell.

This is not a breeze that blows; this is wind. The creek's splashtraffic, the beech leaves crinkly and fluted, these things are less than things today and I'm less than that to be saturated with them.

Later, some days later, I sit at a clearing bordered by pines, holly, cedar. It's colder, seasonable. A mockingbird hops on a branch of a cherry. It looks, preens, looks some more. It seems to rest, wait, plan its next move. Stays, the bird. A long accordion of cirrus trawls eastward. In the same direction two dove streak. Gasoline smells mingle with the gritty, boiled rice smell of wet ground. A squirrel stops on its descent of a pine. It stares at me, raises a forepaw. Just three points bind it to the bark. Perhaps the squirrel's large ears keep it balanced. Were its tail not twitching it would resemble a toadstool.

What the eyes see and the mind see are in such curious contrast some days. All the senses relate with the oddly embodied grace of a devilish instrument. Pluck the note of taste and the skin behind the knees heats up, even as the fingers numb. Such is February here, the biseasonal month, the cleanse. And it always, even in August, is a little bit February. So many things going on at once and nothing, too, wind in the pines' crests, mockingbird rattling, sun breathing into a million points of shine.

Many are glad for numbers, months, days, ways to keep track of time. Many are glad, too, for ways to lose track. I have a little. I leave the clearing and cross the parking lot. The river's giving the sky a slowly tremoring version of sky, and greyer and glossier both. Boils resemble the pattern of lichen on stone. The water has fallen. Along the edge of the river is a line of wet wood and mud, a line of wet on the logs and trees as though they wear stockings.

The birds are excited; their maelstrom contrasts with the river's sluggish course and the lack of wind. The notes combine with haste, pitched with the sweetness of a tart fruit.

I watch a puny bird descend a network of vines and limbs not four feet away. The bird has yellow markings on its head and on its wings. It pops more than bounces, oil on a wet skillet. I try to see it as though nothing ever had a name.

When I crest the river's bluff, there's a heron downstream and across with a large fish in its beak. The heron tries three times to swallow the fish and fails. I'm too far away to see what sort of fish, but the heron strains to lift its head. Before it jerks upwards in attempts to swallow the fish, the bird holds the fish and its beak under water for a long almost-minute as if to cleanse or lubricate or give the fish occasion to squirm into a position— perhaps death, that stillness—from which it can be more readily swallowed. The heron flies upstream when I move again, giddy bumbler, for a closer view, and at once the spring peepers speak up, their chorus undulant and raspy, some homage to activity underground, growth below the surface, of roots downward and outward and of stems to the surface.

Time feels rigorous, vigorous with openings. Making sense has rarely made such little and vast sense. I stand now tasting lichen and walk into a day no different than it's supposed to be and changing. One foot (breath), the other (next). Pause, walk some more. *Coon crap, deer crap, fox scat, owl scat.* I go on, sink with it, rise.

March
Dilations

I set off for another walk with no place in mind. *This is my life at the foot of the mountains.* If my steps become a kind of hope, kind of complaint (bump and grind), so be it. *To the coastal plain, my life, to the sea.* I go on, follow my feet, some rhythm established by the sound of the boots as I step, the lay of the ground, the blood beginning to flow.

The woods seethe, swaddled in immanence, promise. A person wearing earplugs could feel the birds' vibrations—of flight, song—and know that winter's on the fade. Here and here, existences between fly and moth. Squirrels, leaf-ruffle. Red glow of maples, nearly all the canopy pocked with budgrowth.

So March marches to the woodpeckers drumming, quiet, now quick. Every day the general hue of things amplifies. The ambient glow grows by decibels, half decibels. I ooze it. With it, of it.

For years, I grew. I grew to such heights and then I came down; it was slow, *a weathering*, and now I'm fertile, they say, and now I'm passing through, they say, and now I'm closer, closer (is it scary?—it is). Spring peepers, chorus frogs, a hawk's screeches. Spring's audible despite the traffic sounds. I listen for new sounds, ones that emerge, such as the jay, and for the ones that have been here all along, beneath perception, wind in broomsedge, the painted turtle's splash as it plops from a log.

And still I know so little, some names of things, some feelings, sensations. I might lose myself here and in that loss be restored. I might, but what do I know. Some mornings are a bright song. Some mornings the sky is utterly clear. I believe every word the days don't speak.

On the pond, green gobs of algae in bloom, mats and mats. Thick and blistered with air pockets, as if the burned skin of some swamp thing. Geese karfle, they karfle and krull.

So March arrives with May on its breath, and I'm a follower once again. I follow my legs. I follow slants of light in bright patches. The woods are an essay my body reads as if directions to some place nobody's ever been or might ever find.

The cedar trees know more about me than I ever will. What freedom. Feels like a blanket has been lifted, the blanket of getting somewhere, saying a thing.

Go on. Nothing is dead in the woods. To rot is to live. To be removed from the cycle of growth and regeneration, perhaps in a casket or a morgue, a jar of formaldehyde, that's the one true death. But even a jar breaks eventually and a casket rots.

To know body as nobody. Sometimes new growth, a certain perkiness in the chlorophyll, pulls, though I don't know I'm being pulled until I've passed the source and am following the song of a bird I don't even want to see so I have a better chance of seeing it. Then, if lucky, I stop and turn to see how I've come, knowing that it won't look the same as it did on the approach.

Here's a decent seepage stream. I turn over a rock, watch the water cloud. The clouds of silt clearing speak of forces at once beyond and within. This is not heaven. This is not a kingdom. This is a walk.

As the silt moves downstream, I begin to see the larvae, the wet leaves, a crayfish, the tail of a salamander as it squirms under an adjacent rock. Carefully I replace the rock to its original position, as if a rock ever has an original position.

They say there was an ocean here, the Iapatos, and that great rivers ran as the ocean retreated and the continents drifted. Where I was then is where I am now. History. Take the cedar's roots entwined with the oak, the creek flowing through them, it's that closeness I need now.

March surges through the canopy, now in the pines, now there across the pond, in more pines. The sound rolls across the woods, and where I sit there's a sound like rain, as if minute seeds were falling, bouncing off the dry-leafed duff. Maybe the sound, a small, general crinkle, is the noise of leaves drying after a night wet with dew.

The turtles have returned to their sunny log after abandoning it when I first walked past. A hundred yards away, they appear as bright, spheric darknesses with neck and head. They must feel a great heat after just a short time in the sun. I suspect the warmth penetrates their shell, as it does mine.

Are their eyes open? Do the turtles blink? Now's one of those blinky mornings, suddenly bright beyond comfort and then cloud-darkened, gusty, and then still, ecstatic with birdchirp or only a distant crow.

I turtle with a vengeance, so determined to see that I'm blind. I want to see with my feet or maybe my belly, but the mind's a brute some days, surly as any schoolyard bully, and older.

Sometimes, though, a moth does its air hop not six feet away (there are many gnats, too), and I'm throttled into shadow, coiled with vines of undeserved grace. I turtle in the pond just by looking at it. I turtle the energy of its deepest feeding midge and promise myself never to apologize for this, never to be ashamed.

What else to say? I walk, sit, turtle some more. I don't stay long. I stay long enough. I want to learn about the interior, but the interior's without. Even the clouds are a gauze some days, silky and warm. Bugs are as active on the stream as the vines are in the canopy. Everything links to everything else. Outer space is inner space, or so says the deer's walking sounds.

March was always frenetic, with lows in the twenties and highs in the fifties, or snow and then seventies. Patches of spring beauties hint at the onslaught of warmer days and brighter blossoms. But it's chilly again now, and where I sit, feet on a rotting log, rump on an oak's roots, creek below and seepage behind, I hear woodpeckers, crows, jays, and running water. Wild ginger, Christmas fern, and young cedars stand over the leaves, the moss, the sweetgum balls. I sneeze, but the sweat bee doesn't mind; it keeps doing that hovercraft dance near my leg.

The way the cedar limbs curve, to stretch my arms, legs, torso, and neck that way, maybe I'd live forever, but I hope not. Dirt's too sexy for living forever and for believing, anyway, that we don't, even as dirt. The knobbed, warty holly, on the other hand, it contains an antidote to arthritis in its boiled leaves.

All the months are patient in their own ways, March no more or less than the rest. Each year brings a different manner to the unfolding of days, weather, and season, the pace of decay and regeneration. My body gets carried away all the time, is quick to assign itself to things. Sad thoughts, sad shadows, the perplexity and poke of pinecones and stuff. So prick my skin with a thousand holly leaves. There's a pile of bones in the duff, or else that's the white of lichen colonizing old, fallen sticks.

Things dilate, dogwood buds, buds on the maple and the hickory and elm. The birds seem to be opening a thousand old doors with their chirping. There's less space for a person to think, perfect. Heron's wingbeats are many sheets on a bed where somebody's tossing and turning; I'll sleep in time with them all night.

I turtle on a fallen pine, the tip of which extends into the pond. There are needles at its extremities, butt ends of needles ragged and brown. Algae in gooey webs hang there, a sign of recent higher water. They could be ornaments in spring's Christmas, all the birds and frogs caroling.

I hope to see a snake. It seems a snake would thrive here because of the pinebark, the needles and leaves, and the proximity of the pond, as well as the earth-pocked rootwork upended by the trees' fall. As much as seeing one, I like the idea of a snake being here, that I'm sharing its habitat. To see a snake would affirm my choice, but when does nature affirm anything but surprise, ambivalence and surprise.

Dead honeysuckle vines still coiled around the fallen limbs begin to appear, as if they weren't there all along. Downlog, a turtle crawls into the sun. The March breeze feels permanent for a while.

I go to the river again. Gaudy mockingbird toots its horn on the far bank. I notice a patch of bedstraw in the twigpile that high water left. The bedstraw has a square stem and a roughness like a cat's tongue. I break off a small length and try to stick it on my jeans. It does not adhere; perhaps it's too young.

Dense green splotched with yellow, purples, and whites of blossoms, the ground—butter and eggs, horsemint, and other things I could say the names of, but then I'd need to stick one in my mouth. Let them be.

How good it can feel to not say the names again, to say them by not.

Small, scattered clouds shiver on the water like eggs devoid of yolk. The river's a drab skillet. I sup from it with my eyes, rapturous as any fool in spring.

One of the clouds shrouds the sun and briefly the river appears brown and deeper and colder. At once I feel the threats and promises of summer, low water, humidity's unwanted bear hugs. I feel it too well. It might as well be one hundred degrees. For a while I have a short nap and dream the world closer, close as the season's first sunburn.

So easy to just go my busy way, but I've just flicked my first tick of spring into the weeds. How could I stop now?

Of this I'm sure: the terrible news of these times, the news untold, the lies, all the machinery of desire, of want (not need), the onslaught of hope, silly hope—it's all here, even here in this late place, cut anew. I bear it, can bear it. Because nobody's lying to me here. Nobody's giving me the runaround, telling me what it means or doesn't to be human, to yearn and serve. There's no show here. Here is a late place, a being, so many, and those who run the show, who bought it or puppet for those who have, they aren't here. I won't hear them calling me a fool for trying to feel this place before it was this place, a late place cut anew. This is the place, the floodplain, where I won't find them at all. Dirt was always old growth anew. The fools, the foolshow, it tries to creep in even now. This is the one place I won't find them at all. Now wood ducks approach from downstream. Go ahead, listen to the volume increase, the volume of their wings whistling, wind through feathers, feathers through wind.

Junky, this stretch of floodplain, and it's growing me. On me, too. I like it. It's here, near where I park for work, and it's useless to industry, valueless in terms of real estate, and all this river birch, scraggly, peeling lepers of trees. There's rain in the air. I walk heavy-lidded, mind as grey as the clouds. Habitat becomes me. Some call it lazy, but living loose, close to the land, a professional wanderer and wonderer is my ultimate career plan.

Damp, the redbud's lavender through this alley of hardwoods. Damp, last year's leaves still fluttering on most of the beech trees. And I won't find the others here, either, those rabid and tyrannical with prescriptions, sanctimony. Even now, the place is a pandemonium, such raucous serenity, especially the cardinals, all done up as if they've been reading the glossies on how to get a mate. Spring can be sickening. How can one walk among so much bark and not call the world cracked, not be cracked myself? Look at the vines in all manner of bend and reach, the moss, the tenderness of the first green on the young mustard plants. What's grotesque begins here. What's graceful begins here, too, and what's in between.

A bug with red wings drifts a few feet from the ground. It resembles a lightning bug. I sit on another old, fallen pine. Could be a bus stop along a mighty boulevard in a city on the decline. I breathe with surprising ease and hear more, perhaps, than I know. What else do the holly trees say with their spines, if not "Bug off." Humans in previous times, perhaps as riddled as us in these days, made armor of the leaves—or so the books tell me. I can, if I forget myself properly, smell their ghosts residing in these very trees.

I walk again. I leave the fallen pine and, swarmy as the season, cross tangles of deadfall, seepage bogs. If I follow something, towards some destination, it's not clear, at least consciously. The clouds thin with shocking quickness. This is where I feel happy with so many pieces of my heart, I don't even know this yet. Nobody's spinning the truth on me here except (accept it) myself. It's bright, the woods a garden (shadow, shine) where earlier it seemed a nuthouse. Instead of demonic totems, the dead cedars look like dead cedars.

I end up where I start. Isn't that how it goes? No, something different. I breathe with surprising ease and hear more than I ever will. "Welcome back," says the holly tree. But the pine, the old, fallen one says, "Get lost."

April
Salamander Dancing

Three redbud trees in blossom before a thick of pines, a timing to them and a voltage that speaks a truth I'm not yet able to hear.

Is there a rhythm to these jaunts now, these encounters? Or less rhythm than inevitability? No plans required, it happens, maybe not every day, that I get out here, if only for a little while—it lasts forever.

And still I doubt it, feel shame for it, for being out here, feel truant.

I sit in a canoe at the head of the pond. A day of contrasts and gusts after a night of rain and the arrival of a cold front. Patches of blue visible between thick cumulus. Everything forceful, as if a person could sit inside a building with thick walls, no windows, and feel the weather's presence.

The pond's shallow here. Scum, seeds, shoots litter the silt at the bottom, a few sticks and rocks as well. Water striders dart along the surface. I feel like running just to keep up. I'm nervous, not yet prepared for deep spring, its color, form, measure. Already it's time to move the clocks. The dark dwindles. It's easier to dwell in the dark. What to do with the bright and giddy days?

I canoe, for one thing. I ride the skins of ponds and rivers, put myself in the middle for a perspective on the edge. And swim, submerge in the liquefied version of previous days. I bathe in the silt.

The turtles are my guides, my companions. The waterbugs, the fish. Let the heat try to get me then, ten feet down, blowing bubbles, amazed by the surface of the water, the light filtering through.

To make the dream the waking, to make the sleep the walking dream: I cruise the world's many mazes. Or not. Bewildered, safe, amazed, confused, hopeful, aroused, whatever it is, I feel good on these jaunts, and better especially during the life between these jaunts (because of the jaunts), which, if this is a story, is one of the story's many springs, tributaries, branches. There are often springs under a river. And trees.

Let them hone me, screw me in, these woods, walks, this sitting and looking around, feeling, trolling with my nerves for what's here as much as for what isn't, making the here more possible, more present, all its essences, proximities.

Another day, and cool again. Okay, love it. Sitting in woods burned over not long ago, sitting in scattered birdsong and wind in limbs. Young trees shake between the pines; they're lit with the lime frill of bud and bud-burst.

The beech leaves rattle without end. Over a trunk a spider has sewn a gossamer lid. Next to it a maple shoot, a young pine, and they shoot through moss and a bed of needles. Mud from antwork rises like a monadnock.

Down by the creek I find a dismembered bird among the spring beauties. The sun warms this grove that later, after dark, will shine with moonlight and frost. As I walk home, the wind disappears. Everything shakes, especially the shadows, with the shuffling of countless beetles and roots.

Meanwhile, behind the parking lot at work, the floodplain thickens. For lunch, I wade knee deep in that grass, body a chunk of tick food. Spires of henbit rear their gangly, purple heads on greencrimson stems thick with juice. Other flowering weeds pepper the grass with white and yellow blossoms small but populous enough to resemble little burnings. There's no smoke save that of birdsong and pollen. Swallowed by so much growth, I leap to a place where the bluff has sloughed, creating a sandy steppe. Smilax vines hangle and tang as if the work of some savant spider with a penchant for spines and a woody silk; that such a critter could exist seems possible on these banks.

The river runs at the lowest levels I've seen since beginning to explore here some months back. River's on another riff now, a rockier one. Logs and rocks dry in the sun; turtles lounge there. I like the reflection of green among the blue of the sky and the trees' brown and olive hues; it reminds me of an old ball of Play-Doh, the colors mixed despite a child's best effort to keep them separate.

Above, a tree in blossom, each flower three burgundy petals in a dangling, labial mug shape. A small tree, smooth-barked and reminiscent of sumac in angle and width. The eye doesn't go to it the way it goes to a sycamore or birch. But the tongue, it directs the eye to the tree, says look. So I do. Hairy-husked and oily, the blossoms look like bat-candy. If I'd never tasted it, I wouldn't in seeing these blossoms imagine such pulp, such sweetness.

Fungus, scallopy growths. Leaf-rot. Stumps and swale and trunkbend, angles. Everything mottled, especially the wind as it arrives in saucerish flumes and then leaves in much the same way. Puny new leaves on select trees are a mottled glow. Peeper and birdsong, bluets and spring beauties, holly, sweetgum, pine, all of it mottled, hues running the entire spectrum, and then some, as though the spectrum's so many cells, dividing.

There's always this music being played, simple but not, and some days I have to join the band: *A green tunnel, the river, a tunnel where green explains its history and variety. Green grows the tunnel here. The river tries hard to ignore it. The river silted with clay, luscious and aware. Hear the birds now tell of green's day. Of green they sing and to the green. Even the oldest, darkest green—of pine and cedar, rhododendron and laurel—hasn't heard it all. The birds sing of green's big days, the roaring times. River riffs, too. History played by bird and by water, by stone and by light. Water thrush, teal. The turtle in the tunnel of song and of green, the painted turtle in the tunnel of song and thrum and green, the painted turtle slick in its shell, dropping off the log as goose, another goose, bends her head, stretches her neck unmoving as if the egg of everything green and not green underneath. The green heron, the parula, the cardinal, the wood duck, the muskrat, and the squirrel. The tunnel turning, revolving. The greening of the tunnel's middle edges is unsimple and yet so. For instance, the boxelder, by contrast, against the boxelder. Or cedar on azalea and the little grove of bluffing constant along the, no, the banks.*

Fern stalks slowly unscroll near the maple's trunk. Birdsong swarms, erupts, little volcanoes in the branches, lavas of breath. Ricochet, the chirps and squeaks, to all degrees. Things are still, mostly. They are quiet and the more quiet it gets, the louder the crows sound, shimpering in the distance. It's the same with the light on the trees, the same volume. Things relate in ways beneath knowing. Perhaps my body's laid out here unfastened by delight's razor for the sun to dry.

March's innocence is April's demise. The woods have nothing to do with me no matter how hard I try. Out of despair and cleaving do my eyes commune with what isn't even here. That rotten log, its cracks and sloughlines. The algae, the moss, the lichen. Were faith a stethoscope I could never hear the activity of bugs inside. Still, how could one not shower so among such showerings, mayflies, gnats, spiders, the water thrush going bob bob and flutey? The sun does blaze on the pond these mornings like some furnace on high. When the air is colder than the water, smoke rises. I have seen it, have called it mist. Have heard the geese, too, and said of the ferns that they gave birth to snakes in the deep past.

All around the woods bugs roam. Ants, black and red, march over and under the fallen leaves. Butterflies and moths spell dizziness with their flight. I see them without even turning my head. Now an ant carries a dead spider onto a stick by my left foot. Busy life!

Of course I wear a hairnet of spidersilk. One can only be so careful. A tick crawls on my shorts. There it is. So I take it and flick it away. It's harder to see the sky now. There are so many leaves. I could say there's another sky now, a green one. Still a few redbud blossoms hang in there, more purple than pink. A strange wasp shimmies across my view upward. Watching it disappear in the maze of leaf, wood, light, I hear a hermit thrush, my first of the spring, and I suck and swell like a tick with those smells, tastes, images, a rush of springs and summers past.

A monarch slips as though on a crooked, graceful track upstream towards the bowl of the seep's head. Everything's crawling or flying or busting into brilliance. For a minute, it's too much. I long for winter's quiet, its stillness, but the minute, like all minutes, does pass.

Gracious, I've just found a four-toed salamander under the wet, silted leaves. Pale brown stripes on its browner body, though they're only vaguely stripes, more long splotches. I hold it, this singular life, this soft scurry and softer stillness, hold it in my damp, open hand and regard it with all the reverence of a child pulling a plate off the edge of a table, discovering gravity.

Life keeps coming. Conversations, glasses of water. Tasks and play and voices. Bodies, tools, buildings, cars. The phantoms and pleasures—failure, joy, hope, sadness, regret—none of it less necessary or entangled than the woods in which I breathe for an hour or so most days.

The beaver have repaired the dams my neighbor tore down in March in order that the pond be filled to spring levels. I bumped into him, Mr. Webb, at work against the beaver, and though I knew better than to mess with habitat like that, I helped, and it was a good hour, a Sunday afternoon, warm. My daughter and her friend caught frogs as Mr. Webb and I took pickaxe to dam, waist deep in muck. The girls squatted in the mud, dirtying the hems of their dresses. They were wearing dresses. As the dams opened and the water drained, they caught crayfish left high and dry on the exposed mud flats. They caught them, giggled, and they seemed entirely solemn too.

I've read since that beaver make decent pets. That separated from their kind, they lose interest in labor. That they respond to names and grow affectionate, missing their owners when left alone. One account spoke of a beaver cuddling kittens once the mama cat weaned them and left the bed that the beaver had earlier abandoned for the mama cat's use. And I've heard of pet beaver that gnawed furniture and wainscoting and the trees and shrubs of the garden.

The dams here at the head of the pond are on either side of an island, one four feet and the other eight feet across. The beaver repaired the dams such that they're larger than before the demo. They back up a creek that's no wider than the distance a healthy adult could jump. The pond makes a shape roughly like a butterfly, wings on either side of a narrow place. I sit at the edge of it, on a maple blowdown. After walking for a bit this dawn, wandering, following drainages into drainages, I ended up here. The log on which I sit presses against a maple tree, presses it nearly horizontal, yet the stress has not stopped the latter from leafing out. A breeze, lithe pollinator, from across the pond shakes its limbs and leaves.

The pond's a mess of scum and low water and muddy banks wormy with goose crap. The beaver have stripped the alder and other shrubs. Hardly visible, the sun through the branches of the canopy, yet I taste its breath and feel it clam my skin. In the times before iron, Northern people of what's now called Canada used beaver's incisors, attached to a wooden handle, to cut bone and carve their antler-tipped spears. Beaver teeth are broad and of soft substance covered with hard enamel, allowing a balance of hard and soft that's necessary for fashioning a good edge.

I listen for a while. It's quiet despite the breeze. Through the dams, a little water trickles. It's getting towards May. The breeze seems to be evacuating the night's cool air, scurrying it off through the woods. The sun has been up for thirty minutes or so. Warmth stirs everything. Little thermals bloom in the shade and at the edge of the shade. I step. It's colder at my feet than at my head. The young maples tremor, and the low branches of the dogwood, a few petals remaining, slough now and then, and some of them do not stop with their sloughing.

Can it be that birdsong, too, adds to the breeze? There's such compression behind the voices and when they erupt a great stretching of tonalities. The range of notes feels equivalent to the range of greens—many, many shades.

The winter-dead Japan grass, so prevalent here (and so many places) in prior days, is hardly noticeable beneath April's flood. As I came through the field to the woods, there were hordes of dragonflies, their graceful traffic in the light. Teale called them "children of the sun," observed that when a cloud passed over the sun, they stopped their flying, as if they'd come unplugged. With heat and sun for over a week, they've had a good run of it.

Mornings and evenings are the jewels, charged times, as water at brink of boil. My body bursts with tick and chigger bites. The itching some memo that I'm a habitat, too, and it gets me into the woods even when there's so much else to do.

At the pond, frogs go chat and other frogs go chort. Two geese kick around. There ought to be a sign here, at the edge of the beaver pond: *Welcome to Frogland.* Not that I've seen a frog today (and I've looked), but their music prevails. Or a sign that reads *Goose Crossing.* Or *Be Aware of Atamasco Lily—They Bite You With Their Grace. Turtles Sunning. Myriad Greens.* Gracious, the wood could be water and the water could be wood. Here ants crawl on my shoe; they make me think of signs.

So glad there are no signs here. There's a breeze, however, and I wonder if the innermost motions of a living tree can sense it through the way the branches and leaves shake, noting direction, speed, coming weather. The beetles in the dead wood, maybe they feel it too.

The shade of a dragonfly over a spider's web, is it a clue of the day's bounty? How that ant crosses the sweetgum nut husk, pausing, changing direction, it speaks to the position of the stars. The world extends towards compression, even worlds unknown. That spider, for instance, black with yellow stripes, on the pine needles, knows the radiance of the needles' coldest hours. How it walks, that spider, deliberate, elegant, as with a confident, terrified hunger.

May
Captivity

May now and the crows continue to crow as though it were any day or season. I hear the flutter of wings and watch the flooded creek, a patch of yellow iris up to its neck in the deceptively still and definitely scum-flecked water, the blossoms soggy, sagging, ablaze.

Two inches of rain to usher in May, and now the sun breaks into a mess of shadow and shine. Atamasco lilies like glasses for holding bubbliness. Atamasco lilies, the Cullowhee lilies, spilling with splendor, May's bounty.

Green heavies, everywhere in the face. Green grows, does thicken and heavy.

Goslings in single file between ma and pa kick to a place near the far shore. The algae that bloomed and grew so prevalent, nearly masking the entire pond, is but a fraction of its original, early-April size. Has it sunk? Has it been washed by the rains over the spillway? It covers the rocks there now, evidence of the torrent. The goslings kick a cribbage of pathways on the filmy covering.

No, may there be no picture, May, and less and less of the getting.

Listen. The airwaves carry in their frequencies a new bandwidth of tremor. I'm trying to breathe this into the solitude of my hindmost tooth.

Such gaudiness, May, such fear and gloaming and glaze. Even as the days distend, the depth grows crowded with an austerity like faith or spiders. Walls of foliage are not walls but hands and tongues and prayer flags that need no touch as I need theirs, passing through them, feeding the ticks, dispersing the pollen.

May, now, and the earth accepts its relation to the sun, the earth and all the places and forces (which are its places) on it, the basins and edges, migrations, assassinations, fornications, it accepts and acts with some harsh and gentle mercy of birth and decay on all the roughage, spirit and flesh and what else between and within.

Look, there's a daddy longlegs and a couple of ants in the leaves now. They've probably been there forever.

Another walk, little forever, this time in a dense cove above the river. In a spiral I move, tromping on mayapple, wild ginger, bloodroot, a kind of raised linoleum of leafshapes freckled with light where the sun finds its way through the canopy. The soil and the leaves are damp. The rotting logs are damp. But there are no morels. Maybe it's too late in the season. The trees here are oak, beech, hickory, sycamore. Morels prefer poplar, apple. I'll have to find another grove, where the poplar grows.

Filled with images of morels, the grooved, brainy cap, flesh-colored and ovate, I notice puffballs, oak fronds, the leafless stalks of mayapple where the deer have grazed. Fruit hangs in the place the flower not long ago shone its rigid pale lemon petals. I sit on a log where young maple, ankle-height, grows, a pair or two of leaves at their peak. A breeze gently ruffles everything. Shadows bend and shake.

The leafy duff tremors just down the log, as though a mole or snake burrows there. Maybe it's a beetle. A spider, striped back and scorpion-legged, crawls slowly, gingerly across a hickory husk. Ants, too, flies, ticks, a bumblebee, a whole metropolis visible.

I sometimes don't know better than to go to the woods with a mission. Morels, even now, when I find them, seem to find me. The laws of discovery are as warped and lovely as justice itself, a beech tree of logic. Look, there's a millipede, black-shelled with a yellow edge. A length of scales narrow and nearly flat, it crawls along the leaves and under them and out again, antennae twittering, maybe fifty legs in sum, or sixty-three. Such a concert of legs and motion. What animal could possibly make of this critter a meal?

Now the millipede rolls itself into a ball. I don't know if it's eating or what. Is it even a millipede? It has yellow dots up the middle of its shell, too. The more deeply I examine it, the more startled I am by a fly when it lands on my knee.

The woods, every time, dress me in spidersilk. Silk clings to my face and some gets in my mouth. I'm tattooed with chigger and tick bites, scented with the lotion of pond water and essence of holly blossom. A walk's a fine makeover.

Here's smilax, cleaver, nettle. A strong breeze begins in the treetops and finds its way to the forest floor, ruffling the webs checkered with sun.

A thick sunbeam lights up a place in the woods on the far edge of the seep, making it difficult to look anywhere else. Something great is happening there, as if there isn't everywhere I look and don't look and cannot see.

Late-spring in the Piedmont is a thick time. The afternoon heat can make summer and summer's glorious, fecund decline very real, more here than imminent.

Always marvels. The cool, scented, moist breeze at morning, chilly nights. The abundance itself is still surprising, winter a not too distant memory.

How much I loved in the barren days to stare at the canopy's joinery, the interweaving of the neighboring trees' crowns. How much I longed for my first swim.

Muggy now. I try to stay on a course parallel to the creek. Deadfall, vines, and webs direct me into the creek, which is low, though sometimes I have to go away from it. Frogs hop into the stagnant murk from mudbars, squarking as they go. Spiders from the webs I now wear crawl on my t-shirt and arms. Sweat beads on my forehead, drips. The air itself seems to sweat. It's hard to tell what clouds roam the sky. Most of the time there's a green sky and songbirds are a kind of cirrus there, or stars, shooting, as if the green was night.

There's a captivity about being in the woods now. I welcome it, the redundancy of green. What else is there to do? I could climb a tree and poke my head out for a vista. But every leaf is its own view, the watershed of veins, network of ridge and sky. The green hearts of redbud leaves throb, even the bug-gnawed ones.

I feel like a spider myself, crawling around on the fat green lady of May, her makeup still perfect in places, but mostly beginning to run. Being is desertion. Questions march in the mind like so many bees. God save the queen.

Whether by birds, falling limbs, wind, or other travelers, all my webs are broken. These times in the woods no longer make sense, but they feel right; to the body, then, they make sense.

Broken, broken, broke, focus is everything. Focus, even broken, is what's here. Everything is here, and virility, and promiscuity, and emptiness. Emptiness, as someone said: the only freedom there is in a fallen world.

Who's to say a cicada won't emerge at my feet, or maybe hundreds of them. How many nests do I pass by or under or over each day? How many eggs, larvae?

A bird—who cares what kind—feeds from a limb low over the creek. It darts down and then returns, flicking its head as if chewing or gulping. On the bank there grows one five-petalled yellow flower. Its stalk is four inches in height, fuzzy, and hung with soft ovate leaves that extend opposite one another, two at a time. Each petal is notched severally, as though whiskered. There's a darkness like purpleblack among its pistils and styles. Nothing bothers it; it seems to bother nothing. It's so steadfast and delicate. If I knew its name, I wouldn't say it. If I didn't know its name, I'd make one up.

May rolls on, erasing itself, as months do. I try to do the same. I fail, walk. Sit, walk some more. Here's a roof shingled with hickory leaves toothed and opposite veined. Here's a cider bug on water stilled by the beaver dam. The bug, a tank, zooms quite well for being so armored.

The leaves are raining. They are letting go of their holdings from last evening's storm. The breeze helps them; gravity helps more.

They sway, too, in the breeze, the leaves. And they make shadows of themselves on themselves. Theirs is abandon and careless carefulness and utter utility all at once and not at all. I want some but know in the needled duff of my soul that I have plenty and will never quit.

Faces in the old cedar stare at all and none of this at all. The faces, cross-gendered as any mushroom, are heavenly, and see.

Water runs in stippled braids where it flows through the dam, the mortar of mud and leaf, root and branch and log. The bottomland is bottomless, as usual.

The honeysuckle says yes, infinite yes with its odor, as though engaged in a discussion of the rainbow that bridged the woods last sunset after the storm, a quickie.

And suddenly the sweetgum tree sends a paratrooper to investigate.

Instinct is famished, says the sudsy, tannin-braced water, to nobody at all.

The birds fuss. They bleat and cackle. It isn't beautiful, isn't restful or ugly either.

Meanwhile, essence is a water plant long endemic to this place.

Big ooze of May sun. Fog lifting. A hawk flying over the burnpile, snake in its talons. The pines in their lavender slacks. Persimmon's chimes all ringing as the dove coos and the mockingbird perches in the apple that a month ago the cedar waxwings poured into, passing blossom parts to one another in a line like the one the clouds make when the fog breaks not with a crack but a coolness in the face. And where are the dragonflies, where in their waiting for that certain degree of light or heat or wavelength, where in their feeding, in the yearning of their bellies, where and in what cribs do they stay, for the moths are trailing so many scents and the lilies are wilting and the deer ticks are waiting or crawling or sucking, the same way the heart pumps, filtering all this in and out, a long pool of flow and moil like a wind beneath feeling gusty and true.

And later the day's slow and heavy by the drainage where the oak lies, tangles of root, soil, moss, vine at its base. Dim fragrance of honeysuckle on the still air. The less the mind works in such weather, the better it knows. Best is a tired body freshened some by a swim in the pond. Some is the word for these days, when summer, which has been hugging us for weeks, reveals that it just won't quit.

The air's a bad breath, a cottonmouth. A drought feels certain, but few are ready to talk about it. Still the cardinals go their merry way, and the hickory, it just won't quit. Such obscene lapping and lolling, hickory's green tongues.

Summer, all its gears oiled, brings another kind of hibernation. It kicks on the autopilot and the bugs and the spiders run the show. Most afternoons, and this one is not exempt, the sky curdles four times over. Maybe it rains. Usually there's thunder, minor promises or threats, carrots in front of the nose.

I like to sit above the pond and watch the sky develop like bad film on the inky dark. I like to sit anywhere. I like to walk, like it all, but outside's the story here, the woods and the fields and the waters, the land the mountains build as they fall to the sea.

I like it but don't trust it, the liking it. It's okay, there's time, a whole life. Now dragonflies hitch up and some of them dive, laying their eggs under water for the midge to eat or not. The green heron does the moonwalk or something over where the alder grew before the beaver stole it. The green heron so dark with its green and gossamer hunger and fletching.

I listen to the legs of bugs scratch the leaves and twigs. Old logs vibrate with beetle gnaw and grub squirm. It's like the world has performed a few too many miracles this spring and is all business and slumber. Lovers after a fest. The wombs stretched. I might jump in the pond now, I might break the reflection.

The water in my ears, then, is right where it belongs.

What awareness does the dragonfly have of the bass beneath the surface, the one with a galaxy for a mouth? Probably it knows nothing of the bass and everything of its habits and the habits of all things pond.

I could say the dragonfly has many thousands of lenses in each eye, that its vision is voracious, delicate, cold, but I would say more by taking off my clothes and jumping in the pond.

The water's a soft hand. The water's a warm hand. It's a cold hand. I squirm in it, caught insect, and the green heron, if it flies over, says deeper with its wings, says smilier and splash.

I don't get the idea, the idea gets me. Water, vestment for heathens and saints alike. The way the light filters through, for instance, only to a certain underneath. Beneath that's another pond, and a pond is mostly soup, a broth or stock, or it's an eye-ball hitched by the nerve ending of streams to the ocean, that moon-obedient brain.

May dunks me again. May the shark, me the minnow. *One, two, three.* Born in this month, I'm born each May anew and older, my meat and veggie charred on its green, spark-dazzled coals.

Dragonflies dab their abdomens in the pond's black. One hovers next to me, turns 180's faster than light. It orbits, too, seems to be guarding me, perhaps from the no-see-ums and mosquitos. Much rises from the muck at the edge of the pond; much doesn't rise but stays in the muck.

Now the dragonfly, sleek and bluegreen, patrols my other side, some traffic-copter. Meanwhile the evening meat market gets busy. Crickets, frogs, birds, it's a scratchy, plucky racket they make. When a bass rising for an insect splunks the surface with a good splash, it seems to quiet everything else for a minute. Then, suddenly, the kingfisher cranks its shriek.

Budding water lilies appear as if mushrooms on a field of shield and filamentous algae. I feel like a salt crystal on a skillet where some mishmash of flesh sizzles. The woods' edges contain all of this like a wall, or like the sides of a skillet or pot. But I get up and walk into them now, from the frying pan into the fire.

And then it happens. The turtles come ashore to deposit eggs in the ground. They stop me in my tracks. Such an intensely private act, how they stand, small muddy holes behind each rear leg teeming with gnats and ants. I watch one. I wait for her head to emerge, if only for a little while and not fully. Her shell, for one thing, is a glory. Dried pond scum cakes there. The forms of her scales crush every can, they are so lovely. I wonder what colors will bleed forth when the shell is wet.

Redbellies, sliders, cooters, painted, I like their names as I like the wrinkles of flesh where their legs and head retract. The flesh itself is worth a measure of worship. The turtle seems more element than animal. Part wood, part stone, part fire, part wind. I see them crawling along the shallows, kicking up clouds of silt as they go. Their life appears to be a delightful one, days on logs in the sun, the privacy of shell, wide avenues underwater. But it's their caution that fascinates most, how fast they are to go under, plop from log into pond at the littlest tremor, as though so attuned to danger and threat that little else can be known.

Caution, yes, but I saw one a half mile up a decent hill from the pond one day. It was the largest turtle I've seen this May. It rested on its plastron at the edge of a gravel road. It took my breath away and then gave it back as a basin and fallen trees.

Time, the clown. Time, the illusionist and the clown and the escape artist, too. The month's ending, but the season's just getting started. Heavy, wet air weighs down even the birdsong. Damp bark, damp duff—storms brew. The woods fester with rot and growth. The morning trudges as though burdened with latent dusks. It might as well be twilight all day, some sleep incubator. The rain doesn't fall, it surrounds. I breathe rain, look in and at and through the rain.

If actual rain fell, it would betray itself. The abstraction of its essence, the rain's, and its inevitable arrival is a powerful broth. What the heck? The leaves rise, they settle, and then they rise again with a sloughing upward like the beginning of a nod. Rocks sweat. The fungus hugs itself.

The beech leaves that hung all winter and fell, pushed by new buds just days ago, darken in the duff, bent and torn and darkened as with moldlove. Bugs are more numerous than time. There's so much movement. Things grow upward no faster than they expand and sink.

These are the heavy days, the air in which tornados breed. I wouldn't be surprised to see a salamander climbing a tree. What I see is a furrowed slope, pocked with the trunks of hardwoods and pines. There are tangles of blowdowns like rowhousing for beetles and moss—rootballs like small hills. Above, a mosaic of limb, leaf, stem, vein. Breathing has never tasted so green.

June
Layers (One Breath, the Next)

The moon's a lazy eye on a face made of cirrus in the shape of a trilobite. It lights the shed's tin roof. The neighbor's beagle barks at it. I glance up at it through the pines as I walk to the pond. The clouds stretch, figures from Münch. The grass looks like blood. The shadows on the grass are clots. It's June now and cooler than the coolest nights of May. The moon's a cold fire. I can hear the bullfrogs speak of its smoke. I can feel the breeze and see the lightning bugs each time they blink. A car honks on a distant road. The night is crowded with shining, all the canopy a colander. It's okay to step on a slug in the grass. It's okay to feel the dew alive with the coolness of quicksilver and to let it silence me and stop me in its tracks; its feet are made of staring, its bones marrowed with seeing through. The mountains that once wore the dewlight wear it still on the bark that glows with the minerals like minerals on the beaches at the bottom of pines, hardwoods, parking lots, water. There's a fledgling asleep in a mess of twigs, and no stirring wakes it. It knows better than to worry, knows enough to mess with knowing better. This was the day's second dawn.

June can be like this. And more stable. None of September's tropical depressions, never so furtive as March. But what matters is less the nature of months, time, or even season so much as being here, present to the minutiae, what's happening, visible and not. The nature of the nature of now. And what's happening behind that, in front, within. All illusory, tricky: now.

Nothing's required, nothing but attention, and even that, one breath, the next. Hickory leaves in mud, Japan grass, a young loblolly rooted in the roots of a fallen maple. There's more than this by the beaver pond, there's less. A soggy feather lies in a pocket of clay, a place where the water ran the last time it rained. Could be a goose feather or from a crow. A slight breeze rustles in the iris stalks next to it. If I drew an oval in the mud beneath the feather, the feather would be a brow. I'd want to be careful with that oval, not to make it so real; it might wink or it might close, and then where would I be?

I'd be here, still, a million pieces (give or take), unbreakable for being broken. I'm free here, all my millions of pieces, to make a claim about anything and nothing, even what matters, especially what is. Nobody's trying to put me together, nobody's trying to get one thing from me out here. For these minutes, I have nothing to offer. I can say anything. Nothing's required of me now, nothing but presence, and even that, one breath, the next. Haze and frog chirr. Deer prints, two plugs in mud cherty and pale.

A dragonfly with four black wings and a white abdomen lights on the log down from where I stand. It remains there, kind of sprawly, a few inches off the beaver-gnawed stump. It's waiting for the light, I suppose. I do not have to wait; the beaver's tooth-work is enough, the way marks on antlers and bones left a little while in the woods can also bear light enough to see. The stump, its curves, possess me, all my pieces. The variety of form astonishes, is breathgiving, from edgy splinterings of gnaw to the deeper roots' soft curves and junctions. Knobbed and nubbined, this stump, goitered and flanked. Its hardness shines forth, a function of its contrast with the mud or the water. It appeals to every encounter with wood and the sound of falling trees. The glare is brilliant, soft and crisp. It might as well be February in North Dakota as the soggy leather of a Piedmont June. Bask,

bask is the word I've been looking for, although it keeps coming out as flux. The dragonfly twitches now, appears warier.

What I say is what I see out here, and I try to say it until the saying of it is another kind of seeing, maybe another. And another. I say what I see and try to see it again in saying it. I mean see as feel. I attend, reseeing. I say what I see and sometimes the unseen—what is felt—comes alive, and always the layers thrill and soothe—stone under leaf, mudmarks from a rainier time, wood fallen on wood, cascading branchwork, wasps, birds chirping far away and many very close. It's the impressions, the myriad swarm of things that riles me up, empties me full. I need this, these little scrambles, every few days at least, need my senses to wander as my body never will, as though along a map only light through a prism could make as the prism shatters against another prism midair.

A smell like cucumbers and cooked squash. A hollow at the foot of a fallen oak, small colony of white mushrooms growing inside it. The crickets could put me to sleep if I let them. The thrush could make me sway.

Summer woods are tidal. I am tidal. Light and noise are tidal. Life builds and slackens all the time. The birds come and go. Just now, two crows harassed an owl to land on a branch within spitting distance of my seat against a tree. The owl seemed calm for its hassle. It made one last display of beak, and the crows skedaddled. For a couple of minutes the owl looked the other direction. I tried to see it without showing my eyes. It looked at me then or at the flesh where I was about to scratch a bug bite. Maybe I should have scratched then. The owl might have felt more secure, as though the sound could resemble the noise of beaks on wood, insects on bark and leaves.

Not true that the longer I stand, the louder it grows. It grows quieter, too. The woods, you see, are tidal. The senses testify, they lie, and the owl is gone, but not beyond seeing: *Everything strung and leaning and flung or cracked and gristled and worn perfect, the smilax, the red oak sinuous and burled, a tossed salad where nothing is washed and all washes; so much discrete and on the way up down low, big up big up; a gurgle of swarm, of pinchers and shitters and throats and legs; it is split at its wholest center, the interior a heapage of edges and wings, where patterns repeat in tongues there are more of than bodies; the lichen for instance on the cedar stump and the moss there, a universe of particulars in the difference between texture and shade; so much husked and peeling and flaked and squirming, a glow and a shadow, a leap a squirm a quiver such weird machineries of sugar.*

One breath, the next, and the days go by, slow and humid, crowded and alive, and now I sit on a stone in a place where there's stone and water running over stone for a square mile or so. It's dark and if it's smooth, the stone is only smooth insofar as the smoothness exposes a more implacable hardness. The rocks are hot with sun. I have to dip my bare feet in the water every so often to keep from burning them. The spider doesn't seem to mind the heat; perhaps it knows too much of the substances that gave the stone its present shape and of the water that scours its edges.

Not now, not here are they telling me how to live, how not to live. The spider needs nothing, not even my regard. There's so much they say, and so well, with sexy, moving pictures, news, tunes, words delivered faster even than the speed of light, the speed of thought. They are saying such things, sure, but I can't accept delivery here. I've given myself a walk, a little time in the woods, some sanctuary. Nobody can get one thing from me here.

I have nothing to offer. I can hear anything, think anything, say anything. Go ahead. I'm coon and coondog out here, I'm pond scum, antler, bug gnaw, mineral, cloud.

If there are names for this stretch of the river, this mess of toothy rock, I aim to forget them. The stones jag at an angle downstream and are mostly triangular or nearabouts. Water braids through and around the rocks, a vast, sinuous maze of curls and waves, tongues and bubbles and froth. River oats, cane, sycamore, elm, willow, sedge (forget the names, forget them), and other woody life root in the sand and loam-tartared crevices. There's driftwood, of course, logs and sticks and lumber, and water snakes slither among it, and a downstream wind gives the leaves a motion similar to the water.

I've been out of the water for only ten minutes and already I'm dry and then wet again with sweat. The sky's an inverted blue bowl littered with popcorn of cumulus. The river's loud, but now and again the hum of locusts. Little else moves but the water, the leaves, limbs, spiders. Earlier I saw a blue heron, but it has gone.

Last winter a friend was canoeing here and saw an eagle. It saw her first. She was holding her boat such that a wave was holding it harder, allowing her to cut laterally, fanning a little spray off the hull's Kevlar edge. In a soft, reliable spot in the wave's trough, she laid back against her boat's rear deck and, gazing upward, saw the bald in a holding pattern twenty feet above her. It was frightening at first, she said, and then so calming as to frighten even more. There are moments like this. Luck, wonder, devotion, chance, they slap us around sometimes.

Accidental, maybe, but we make ourselves receptive to grace, or else.

The water sings a hurrah here. Brown water, brown with silt of last evening's rain. Lord, how it scrambles. It falls, the rocks say so. The water on the rocks, the friction and filling in—

if I listen softly enough, I might hear it for weeks. It could run over me, bathe me even when I'm running errands, pumping gas near the headwaters of a distant tributary. Someday, years and miles later, I'll smell this water evaporating or taste it condensing with the next rain or the night's dew, and it will bear me, bear me through even greater losses than I can imagine now.

With each breath, the next, June grows thicker, the woods more full. If I look any closer, it feels like I'll disappear.

Is there such bounty that the raptor can afford to set the catfish loose from its talons, to leave it for dead on a rock in the river, clawmarks pink and festering in the June sun? There is such a bounty.

For instance, the young cedar, a scraggly curvature of growth, holds forth. Spiderwebs in disuse stick to it, frayed and matted. It could be exhibit A in the explanation of gangly. It could be the ganglia of the wood's lungs. Pine needles brown and crisscrossed tangle in its dense, frizzy, aromatic greens. It's one more little tree. It has changed my life just by being there in the shade.

Does one thing in these woods give a hoot about being good? Does the cedar wish its seed had set roots over by the stones where the soil tastes better? Does the soil taste better? The wasp there, that wasp's where it is. Fate and being are a strange playdate.

The rotting, the growing, the going by, that's it and so on.

And now that spider going across a long strand, gracious. I have a little time. I'm going to walk around and feel the woods as they are, as I can. The other work can wait, and be better for it. Dowse, go ahead, man, dowse the vibe of a few of the things you see, and fret not; you'll still get to heaven or wherever the hell you plan (or don't) to go. Always these woods within minutes bring me closer, the ordering, the sounding of my breath (the next), my regard, to everything else I do and hope to do.

Each breath a seed set forth, a seed brought in. I try to find harmony, simpatico pattern. The seeds will be okay.

There's a dogwood downslope and the sun on it like a dirty grin. It's a different tree every minute. I don't see it grow, but when I return to this place I might see that the dogwood has grown.

Is it the returning that's holiest, is it the seeing things again?

There are these jaunts. Thirty minutes, an hour. I take it slow, try to get lost, try to see. It's easy enough. There are woods in the Piedmont, scraggly and fragmented woods, behind most every auto parts store. Woods, histories, dramas. I walk, pause, poke around, walk some more. Nothing new, nothing remarkable. Remarkable is all around, and it's time to let it inside.

Or it's time that I'm after, or the way the light's changes can contain time, and how those changes spark so many fires. I want, certainly, to be burned. I want to stop time while letting time do its thing. I want to dance, be spun, spun, all my pieces, and spun some more. Be spun till all my pieces are small with vastness, a kind of infinity, a zilch, some spun way into the outermost of the innermost's mysteries.

Once in a wet time, years ago, a man sat by a spring at the edge of a field. It was dusk, winter. He'd been spying on wood ducks when with a whoosh a big soft strength brushed his forehead. He felt anointed then, as he'd felt most every time in the woods by something strange or mundane or nothing but being there. But that time it was dramatic, funny, too. The heron—no goofier, lovelier, holier bird—sensing him too late whacked his forehead with its wingtip as it banked that tight curve and flew away.

Now what about these dragonflies, how they appear heavier in the air than when they land. Their flight a weighty motion. Are their wings hinged to flutter up and down or is there an angular sidelong way to the quick stitchings?

Several of these fast, elegant insects glide over the pond's backwater. They dart, hover, dart and turn and hover and dart and land on a limb and dart again or stand. One dips into the water, kicking up a splash of several drops, and then repeats this action a dozen times, opening its legs on the downmotion, hurling the drops onto the pine needles and leaf-wet mud.

The water's murky. Bubbles erupt on it, break, send rings. The banks are bluffs of a couple to several feet in height. On them, roots dangle over a strata of pale clay. There are numerous logs and limbs strewn about the creek and the land on either side of it, many of them pocked with the marking of beaver.

It's evening and hazy. A pale light dapples the water where it filters through the trees. Birdsong and cricket-chirr is general, and a wind high in the trees makes a rainstorm feel very possible.

A big frog emerges, its two eyes anyway. I try to watch it but keep going to a sunlit pine reflected a foot behind the frog. Suddenly a whitetail prances through the woods upslope and then out, out beyond any line of vision.

Another dragonfly with a green head and blue body splashes the water. Some of the damp lands on my shoe. Wild to watch the bug fly in reverse. Yet another dragonfly appears. It watches the former and then dives at it. They collide and fly away. Now a yellow-bodied one shows up and dips, the entire motion circular with a diameter of six to eight inches.

It's evening. Even the ferns seem to sweat. They hover. And I hover, too, having come to the water again, having had to, it's who I am. This is the place. Nobody's telling me who or how to love out here. Nobody's messing with my heart. Good's no issue because everything is. Nobody says come to our church, come to our church and worship with us. Nobody's telling me what to eat, what not to eat, to grow up, fix this, buy this, open that, talk to so and so, take a pill, or to get a better job, better friends, better soul. There's nothing confusing here. The confusion I feel out here is a balm. The woods, waters, any woods or waters, are the place, my home. Don't even say visitor, trespasser. The deed to wonder is always open, everyone owns it. There's nothing truant about this. The water is slow, cinnamon-colored. The elder in blossom, great globes of cream along the banks shaggy with Joe Pye weed, yellowroot, assorted vines, Japan grass, and thick, leaning boxelder trees. And that tangle of logs on the far side, it could be the beginning of a raft or just the end of some prior beginning. Genesis is the world's game. In origins are endings where things kick off.

Who doesn't feel the earth spinning most in summer, when a general dizziness is the rule? Earlier, walking, I closed my eyes for a different view. There was a spider on my cheek, its web smeared on my face like a mess of kisses.

Sometimes, depending on my ears, I hear the crow, or I hear the quiet of the bugs. The wind is the earth's belly laugh. One breath, the next, and the sky is always making wildly, the water too, especially in summer. Small fish patrol the water just below the surface, appearing and slipping out of view. Bluegill? Smallmouth? The light, too, is riddlish, and everything's graceful, raggedly so, with this foraging and being foraged, and I might still even hear the crow.

July
The Inner Banks

July the fourth and a silent thunder parades, banging a more silent drum. I taste footprints on the air. Yonder the green heron curls in flight towards another landing, another fishing hole. Soon, I notice blue heron at the far reach of pond, where the creek enters beneath a curtain of foliage. It stands there like a letter in a word somebody began to write but never finished. It stands there in a fatigue of rest and stillness.

Somewhere water sizzles on hot rocks, could be within the clouds that seem to ignore the land with a ponderous passion. Every moment and the one that it extinguishes is an invitation to a drowning. Regrets only.

A pewtery glaze to things. Rain that fell overnight hangs in the air. Dark clouds and a mingling of bright thereabouts, then shiny, now sloughed. Okay to watch the white disc of sun appear and disappear on the pond's grey and brown flatness. Okay to watch the water striders skitter as the ripples of a fishslap near the far shore reach this one.

High summer is a graceful slumber and a quickness like hurt. It's not a horror of feeding and mating that inhabits these days. Or it is. I don't know. Or I do. The trick is to not know so well that I do. Many rings—of wake, of flight, weather, murder, birth—ooze outward even as they spiral closer, crossing orbits.

The sun bugs out, hazy, diffuse. A clip in my step as I enter the woods near the beaver dam, spiderwebs an invisible omnipotence. I like words but like woods better, especially wet, dripping ones early in the morning. Isn't even early now, but sometimes the woods feel early all the time. From my knees down is lost, a shallows of Japan grass, sweetgum, vines. Nothing eases the mind like a hawk's call, so breathe it out, please, breathe it into all the world's pain, fear, hurt. Something arch and entirely focused about that ascension, hawkvoice. It grows me wings for a minute or so, not that I can admit yet that I know how to use them.

A dog barks in the distance. The crickets are a sounding. In the end, such depth isn't to be believed, *it is to be breathed.*

A thrill like floating in knowing nothing at all but what I see. A kind of calm breeds in it, a kind of calm like an opening, another kind of vision. To even speak of it is a betrayal.

The lichen on the fallen maple grows outward like so many blades, a serration. They resemble ferns and oysters and scallops. Waves of growthlines etch the lichen, each a different shade of white, grey, green, violet, yellow; they are like the relief of a steep ridge on a topographic map. I don't tear the lichen from the bark, but in wanting to, I notice that its feet or base roots beneath the bark's crevices. A strong fastening the lichen has, a good hold.

Down the log the lichen is larger, size of my palm. Here they range from nearly invisible specks to fingernail and ear size. Of course, I'm terrified of something and it isn't them.

Here's a river under dark clouds. I watch the clouds progress against the stillness of a boxelder rooted along the bank. I hope they'll bring rain and with it a measure of cool air.

My arms rain. Flies and a butterfly drink these salty drops. A small butterfly, much like the spring azure in size and shape and motion but slate-colored instead of lavender.

From where I sit on a fallen hackberry, the river's hardly visible. The Joe Pye weed's chest high and towers over the Japan grass, barring any good look at the river. Here and there are glimpses of muddy water and leaves floating. Frogs fiddle with their rubberbands and the sun appears briefly.

The clouds are more diffuse than when I first sat. I watch the butterfly that earlier licked my arms (and tickled them). It stands on my hand, opening its wings and holding them open. It has three black dots with white specks in them and yellow for a border. The markings appear to be the doodlings of impulse herself. They lie on wavy lines of brown then grey, six lines like growth rings on a tree.

I can't tell if the butterfly's licking the caulk off my finger or the sweat. It nuzzles between middle and index fingers on the hand that holds the world. Do I hold the world, and with only one hand?—it's so, but only if I grip gently enough, letting go the grip.

The river's adobe-colored in the sun. Two logs stripped of bark and limb by higher water lie along the far bank. How comforting their horizontality in this landscape of up and down, most things jockeying skyward for sun.

There's such a thickness in the woods now, such a luscious slathering and a filling of green. If chlorophyll has a smell, which it must, it's sour, I suppose, and frumpy, some figment of humus and mint.

The clouds of late-afternoon congeal with a grotesque blossoming not unlike the woods with their spines of branches, shadowy stump-pocks, and vinetangles. And then they are somewhere else, the clouds—everybody knows this—and the sun is a filigree, a little skittishing on the leaves' undersides as the river tries to give it back and does, though differently.

The river again, the river always. Behind me a muskrat gnaws on something, its head just out of the water, its forepaws holding that something to its mouth. It looks at me looking at it and doesn't seem to mind. Crickets whirr, a robin spits a musical slinky down a staircase of glee. Downstream a beaver whaps its tail against the water just as the cicadas subside after a heavy refrain. Yes, this is the river again. A yellow caterpillar with frizzy yellow hair and black spikes walks along my knee as I drift in a leaky canoe midstream. The beaver swims a little closer now, and now a slap of a fish as the caterpillar that I flicked from my knee becomes a meal. Everything's still and everything moves or's about to move, maybe pounce. It's dusk, summer. I hear a truck cross the bridge where three guys and a lady watch their bobbers. My old bicycle is stashed in the weeds there, near where I stash the canoe bought for fifty bucks back in the day, a sixteen-foot cruiser with more years on it than length. The boat leaks just slowly enough for short jaunts like these, enough for me to get a fix and get on back.

Yellowroot grows along the banks. It has such an elegant bend and ruffle. Boxelders grow over the river, messily limbed and not a few of their leaves yellow. The region is not officially in a drought, but it flirts with one. There are enough thunderstorms to keep the water table sufficiently full.

The banks here are three to four feet in height and busy with roots. The roots hang like stalactites. It I had a wider boat, I might stand and see the big bass that patrol just beneath the surface. Walking the banks, I've seen them, slow lunkers moving with no movement, creatures of light and dark, of gills and meat and bones and a heaven, this heaven maybe, beneath.

A film lays thick on the river. It has a syrupy aspect and gives the sky that spills on it a grainy, platinum look. The sky's a narrow and curved band on the river, like milk poured on a dark, level place. Downstream, two trees that lean off opposite banks bridge the sky's reflection.

This is the dead water upstream, but the cicadas don't know that. They never will. That is a fine thing. They keep screaming their hearts out, for a mate I guess. Do they notice the thunder when it rips open the air as though a cloth? Their noise continues at intervals that I cannot tabulate. Now the sound in one area of the canopy kicks off, now from another place as the former place is quiet. Seems the sounds come from the pine now, but the canopy's crowded and it could be the black oak. Raindrops begin to slap the leaves. They are small and gentle and few reach the river. I watch a grasshopper swim from leaf to leaf. The river's a mosaic of green and yellow leaves that have fallen. It's a struggle the grasshopper makes, appears to be one. I turn my head to scan the sky for lightning and more ominous clouds, only to hear a quick gurgle at the river's surface. The grasshopper isn't history, but its history's commingled with a fish now, just as mine is a part of both of theirs. Is this serious business?—it doesn't feel like it now, but who knows about the afterlife, whatever that is or isn't. With dazzling quickness, lightning stitches up what the thunder just ripped open.

I paddle back to the bridge. The thunder and lightning have passed. The cicadas are quiet, but maybe I can't hear them now with the sound of the rain. When it stops, I'll stash my boat and bicycle home. For now I watch a swallow snatch bugs from the air at the edge of the bridge joists. I let the rain bring up all the rivers in me, as well as those, like this one, that I never expected to soften my blood. Really, it is much less deliberate than this. I hear the rain stop. I hear it start again, slapping the jewelweed and the vetch.

It's to a place at the edge of the river where I come when the world's emptiness feels too full. The jewelweed hasn't bloomed but is milky with juices, a salve of sorts. I see a number of them, a little colony tucked against a birch that's nearly strangled with grapevine. There are a few Christmas ferns, too, and the barred owl puts out its eight hoots in typical barred owl fashion. Maybe there's a frog slapping about the mud, there is a frog, and a bowl, an old milk jug tucked in the cutbank, light breaking through the canopy, rendering a sulfur glaze that's slightly roseate at the edges where the shadows start and the reflections. It's another day, close to sunrise on a summer day already hot but cheerful with breeze. I may not have any patience for heaviness, woe, etc., but still it is there and I feel it, have to. But how to speak of it when a caterpillar on my knee tells me that emptiness, whatever that is, is empty again, but only for a little while, like the leaves there and the vines curling around other vines. Because how soon emptiness gets bored and turns to nothing, the nothing that is the sound of a snake sliding into the river and me, maybe, thinking of Queen Anne's lace along the roadsides, the orange embraces of butterfly weed.

Another morning. The sun up, firing its acetylene. The bluff lit with a strobey reflection, so many blinking, amazed eyes. I drift by the big outcrop, a habitat of moss, weeds, shrubs, ferns. A good-size cherry stands over the granite, a tree with unusual symmetry and grace in the forking of its five-tiered canopy. It must be seventy-five feet high, its roots growing under the river. If I were a root, I'd like to live under a river.

The outcrop could be a fist reaching from somewhere deep, somewhere fiery and full of longing. Lump of stone, beigepink and lime.

Suddenly the birds grow very vocal. Something to do with the sun, maybe, or the fact that it feels like rain, is slightly cirrus and cool. I dip my hands in the river and press them to my face and look at the river again. On my hands the river smells vaguely fungal with that typical river aroma. Things glow tenderly with the cirrus-filtered sun. Leaves appear yellow where they are green.

The river drifts, or the breezes in it, on it, drifts the canoe and me closer to the rock. I haven't noticed the angular strikes of quartz running vein-like a few feet apart. There's a hankering in me to scramble there, just to sit on the rock, really, not trying to feel the pressure it's known. But the canoe is comfortable enough and the sun bathes me slumberous.

I can't stay out of the canoe. The buoyancy, the floating. There's a slippery motion of bugs where I drift; it isn't a dance but a frenzy, a graceful one defined by a utility I don't know but may understand. The river's muddy. Current where the water has been for a time slack. A middle of the night thunderstorm filled the rain gauge to the inch and a half mark. It fills now the river pretty good too. All the shrubs and trees along the banks sag with rainweight, the boxelder, jewelweed, the poke and sourwood and sweetgum. The air's refreshing with the damp, and though it's hot, nearly nine in the morning, a fresh coolness permeates everything.

The canoe bumps a log at its bow and then spins slowly backward so that I see upstream the milky blue sky over a corridor of foliage splayed with as many greens as God has ears. A branch russet with death extends across the river. It draws the eye with the same dark mystery of a scar or the silken nest of caterpillars in the sourwood, leaves dried and wilted there and trapped and gooey, though shiny, too, where tangled raindrops hold licks of sun.

Odd lines everywhere I look and dashing colors. Strange breezes in my belly. See those beams of sun laying an angled rectangle of shine on the cutbank where the dominant tendencies are up and down, right angles or nearly so, long horizontal flowmarks and the hanging of roots.

Beer cans float bottom up near a hummock of jewelweed. I see one blossom among the dozen plants and many yellowing leaves. I love to touch the jewelweed pods late in the summer and watch them explode.

The cardinal lobelia has already exploded, a deep, scarlet tower of blossoms. Two of them stand along the downstream, and it appears they have never ignored a thing in their entire life.

These are the Inner Banks, those of the Piedmont and Coastal Plain rivers. Upper Banks are the mountain streams and rivers. Many know the Outer Banks.

But names are names. I'm here but I still have a long way to being. It's okay. Time will take me. Look, sweat drips from the air itself. Such is summer. If there's a Piedmont in me, if there's anything in me, it brims with thunder and the rasping of locust.

And so on. I drift once more in the old canoe, trying to see something and maybe feel something, too. Nobody's got their wiles on me here. No one's sucking on my soul. For instance, there's a tangle of logs, and very few have bark anymore and are a greenish brass and cream color. Leaves hang or splay flat on the nooks and in the hollows. It's not a shabby fence the logs make.

The air cools, more rain imminent, thunder growing in volume and frequency. Nothing I could breathe now would make it as it is now or would be to another. The pokeweed's a skinned neck. The light on the river extends inward and sideways. See, the baby katydid on my leg is ripe for flicking. Maybe it'll fly.

Summer's heaviness never leaves, it just turns weightier and invisible for a little while.

TWO: (RE)UNBECOMING

August
Silt

I'm getting somewhere. I have to believe this. I have to keep coming back to see where it is that I might be getting. Piedmont says, you have gotten there. Piedmont says, you have so far to come, so you come and come. Back I come, forthcoming. So much to lose. I have to lose so much, even hope. In order to see I must lose it all, everything I thought I knew, every way I went through the days, all the quenches I learned for fear. To shed the skins, smash the lenses. Even my words (these words?) are lying to me. Even my breath is going to a place that isn't real. Nowhere was always part of getting somewhere. Who are you? And where? I need this. The ache of joy that pierces everything. The way the limbs dance, their quivering choruses of nod and shimmy. Less is it need so much as breathing. I'm dirt, if that, best if less. Don't be hemmed by the noise. Life doesn't always begin with birth. The dark is often the only light. Thick could be the first knowledge of empty.

July drifts into August. A kind of rain, a kind of bleeding. I try to slow down enough to keep up. One day a box turtle stares at me, markings on its shell the color of mullein blossoms. Now plows out of the way, now stops to stare again with determined eyes. One redorange blossom from the trumpet creeper vine lights the woods just beyond the turtle. The blossom could be made of wax or leather. The woods are damp. Fungus stands or lies broken among the sweetgum nut husks and leaves. It's cool, low sixties and fresh-smelling, as though September has showed up early. There are always days like this in August, and they are always strange.

Another day I might prefer the nettle to the smilax, but not today. The birds, smilaxing, are vocal, their song a kind of vacuum, being in the round. My ears ricochet from peep to chirp, touch all compass points. The locusts sound tired.

The woods smell like rot. Reflections of trees and sky, shadows and shine, stain the mud-stained river's surface. The river is thirty or so feet across and slow-moving. One rock stands visible in the river, exposed piece the size of a crib mattress, but who knows what's underneath, what size and being.

Some acid seems to leave my body and especially my brain as I walk. It leaves through every pore, breath, and passing thought. I feel like a hunter whose prey is another self, one buried not deeply but with cunning and luck. The only weapon is a longing powered by the powder of calm and grace's spark.

The smilax contains the history of every swimming lizard. I'm climbing the mushrooms that I walk too fast to see. This is the exit I once passed into the world through. What lies on the other side is another side. The poison ivy vine is prolific, too. Leaves rot. A fish, a bream, lips the river's surface near the squirrel's nest. The jays go back and forth. Bubbles rise, break. Silt settles.

Earlier I went about my days. Now they haul me along. This was the secret of the buttonbush and the ferns.

Meanwhile, amoebas of foam drift by the mud-stained boulder. They speckle the river's surface with pale mottlings. The water is clouded but clear as with a film, and it quietly courses around the boulder. Only a water strider breaks the glass of the river's smoothness. No fish lipping flies, no falls, dimples, pourovers, creases.

Upstream and down is another story. The river curves and bends through the clay bluffs. I can only see fifty yards sourceward, and downstream's windier yet.

The sun lies low over the far bank, a milky shine through the third-growth hardwood. Cirrus are as fish skeleton in the one pocket of sky. There's a chemical smell to the water as though hassled by detergents or chlorine.

A squirrel chuckles just as I'm taken by the svelte elegance of a stump near the water's edge, some ogham in its lines. Stump seems so damp as to be a monument of soil, very little wood left in its cells, something of wings about it, like those angel wing shells that sometimes wash on the beach. Probably a good home, lovenest, battleground for various critters.

Movements are sudden and brief, a soft splash, a thump, a crinkling. Around the bend upstream water breaks, the one constant sound above the pulse and whine of crickets.

With each moment and fraction of moment the pattern of foam on the river changes. The single pieces of foam shift in shape as well. They are not thick, but they are dense, a conglomerate of bubbles. Their motion resembles a pilgrimage, souls streaming towards some nothingness so graceful and great as to be magnetized or just alluring. Bubbles in circle pattern allow one unit of foam to resemble a number of persons holding hands. There's a hollow place, a browngold dollop of water in the middle of the white.

Silt has gathered on a submerged slab of stone, and on it are grooves, the trails of larvae, stonefly perhaps or salamander. No, when I kneel and reach to explore in the shallows there, a crayfish darts and turns, claws forth. I see that the marks are not hers either. A black thing at the end or beginning of one trail turns out to be a snail, a snail the length of my thumbnail, a fleshy mass filling the hollow of its shell.

Snail doesn't say, Let the tropical storms arrive. The storms do arrive—Bonnie, Alex, Chris—each with its own character.

The rain splashes up an inch or so when it hits the river, perfect circle of its wake already dilated to a diameter of four inches by the time the splash subsides. The world's miracles are exact, if not random enough. But they have a motion that seems entirely traditional, ingrained.

The river is the color of an old leather suitcase. It's slow here. The rain makes it feel slower, almost still. I've always loved swimming outside in the rain. Now open my eyes, see the surface, little bursts of activity so formful and constant.

What was drizzle is now a shower. I can feel the regularity of its falling and splashing. What seems to be a faster pace is only more rain falling. The world may not be slow or exact or even, for that matter, the world, but it is regular.

There's a spider on my arm telling me something else. There's a thick bundle of poison ivy dangling from a hairy-looking vine attached to the next boxelder down. The cardinal lobelia will not blink. It is watering. A branch falls, exciting the spiders beneath my skin. Or are those little birds?

I watch a leaf quiver in the cross-hatched pulse of a raindrop's wake, probably an earlier drop knocked from its place on a limb or leaf. There are a lot of yellowbrown leaves floating or half floating on the river. More of them fall. When I look up at the trees everything is green or else it is yellow. The locust fires its jambox, says yellow, but the world confirms nothing. I love it anyway, love it every least way and moment I possibly can turtle, can bug, bird, fish. Even persistence is haphazard in a consistent way. Who has fallen like rain, made on the river a million perfect circles? Or even one?

Downmountain the river is a muddy fist blooming, tearing at its banks, exposing roots. It stinks of runoff. The plain style of dry days is dead. Nothing is flat and hardly a nuance dances now. All baroque and swollen. Seeds and nuts litter the ground. There, simply there. Soon they'll be gnawed, eaten, digested, or picked up and who knows what then.

I know the seasons are not the Piedmont. The seasons are the Piedmont's. What is the Piedmont, America's most lived-in region, *mountain-foot*, place of succession, secondary succession—soil building, soil retention—post climax. The trees know. Ask the trees. They are the voices the seasons use to tell their stories, sing their tunes, and the breeze knows best their complaints.

Everything swims. Even the lichen holds its breath, comes up gasping. There's no other side, no far bank. The day is erosion and sprawl.

So I sit, soaked with sweat and the wet kisses of leaves. Past all eventually, summer's nectar ferments. The sky is goldenrod, ironweed to the west. A yellow warbler hops and flits from branch to branch in a dense stand of mountain laurel, sweetgum, oak. Lichen covers the limbs like a kind of bark. The bird has eyes of opal, a kind of void in them, swallowing space.

Meanwhile, the mountain keeps giving itself to the river. Don't say one thing about generosity. Rain is cloud spit. I am not coming up for air either. The trees are chainsaws. They are slicing up the names for things. Here is some of that sawdust, and it isn't green and it isn't brown. It is flight, it is landing. Here is a leaf.

I paddle in the August dusk, air a heat-drenched lover after a feast of flesh. It hardly slumbers. Crickets are as goose pimples on its flanks and limbs. They purr, echoes of screeches from brighter greens. Of course they are invisible. They're behind the eyes. They nibble at the ears. The river's wakes grow abdominal, silent with vast communities of spiders, trilogies of silk.

Something about the Piedmont that lets me speak, that gives me voice, even if this is nerve damage talking. *Planet damage?* Look, an empty head with too much room for wandering is the sky. Come now, mist, be subtle again. My canoe is too long, still. It leaks but floats me finer than any flying.

The flood has browned the nettles on the banks. The slopes shine with an earlier swelling, a peak, an ebb. Unclear runs the river now and slower, if at all. It shivers with landings, puckerings, a curdling of fins. Heads bob. A wake grows. Who can speak for the interior thick and green like moaning? Beyond, the river oats thick with seed. The tail rises. Lately gets busy again. The tail slaps, each nook vine-tangled or not descends into shades of darkness and the glows and sloughs of cooler heat.

I lately visited the cedars in the grove by the abandoned speedway. How stringy and purplish was their bark. And green with moss. The strings, when they peeled, hung from the trunks like the markings of a distracted whittler. Not until a height of thirty feet did needles grow on the branches. A dense barrenness, that cedar grove. Was prickly, too. I walked carefully so as not to poke an eye. But the eye gets poked. The feet were happy, though, the ground soft with needle, sphagnum, ferns. Few shrubs or vines grew there. It was a cedar grove seeded twenty or thirty years ago. A lot of spleenwort, the occasional maple sapling and holly. Weeds tolerated it, too, their fruit cropped by deergrazing.

There was owl scat beneath a triple-trunked beauty of a cedar nappy and spiderwebbed. The scat was dry and grey and soft as though with mouse remains. There was a skeletal aspect to the stand of trees as well, dead limbs like so many ribs. No wind moved the cedars. If there was movement, as there must be movement in anything dead or alive, I could not discern it. Yet beneath, an array of roots like a giant golf ball torn open, rubberbands broken from their compressed roundness and splayed now in a myriad fusion and unspooling.

I sat a while beneath a tree and heard the occasional jay. Geese passed over, though I hardly saw them through the canopy. Of a cedar's needle what can be said? That it is barbed, that it can be forked or not, that fallen it yellows more than browns, that to see it fall requires no certain prayer, that it is a rough tickle on the skin, that it is a kind of skin, that it is buoyant, tanniferous, green; that it whispers hints at the shape of the grain, that even when nibbled it says so little.

The canoe couldn't care less. I paddle it, slip through a shower of leaves, yellow and brownmottled hickory, hackberry, and maple leaves falling in a breeze. Upon landing they drift, glow, float, host dragonfly, spider, shadow, and light. Their stems sink as though rudders. Their skin seems unabsorbant. The river, stained with itself, is a dot to dot of their peculiar shapes and pigments.

Leaves fall in August. The maple is gold-streaked here and there. By now, it seems that all greens tend toward blues. A kind of purpling, August, because red's everywhere all the time.

So the river has foliage now. It always has limbs; indeed it is a limb, the river, in the tree of a larger river, one more in the ocean's forest.

My eyes go to mimosa, its delicate sway in the breeze, the way it hangs over the river, the way it touches, passively, the air. The breeze blows the canoe against the bank where poison ivy, nettle, jewelweed, and sedge reach their flood-stained, bug-gnawed glory. Or is it sadness? August's is a feisty melancholy.

Morning, the river holds the sky carelessly. The water is no longer high but it isn't low. A river is no richer in flood than it is in drought. In drought it exposes itself, its bed, its edges and hard places. In flood it grows obese yet graceful with devour, slap, cluck. If floods reorganize, so does a drought, the world a mess of constant remodeling.

I wonder why the oak is dead that extends from the bank, five or six years old. The beaver might be responsible, the water too, the bugs.

Once I was dead and now that I'm not, people look at me funny. *Leaves fall in August.* They say I have problems. *Issues.* They do not know how to read me anymore, if ever, as if I breathe another air and out of that air form new translations for things that are, things that seem.

Even in August, even now, the leaves do fall.

As though the air I exhale is not the same air I once exhaled, as though the air has too much yum in it now, too much being.

I don't hang on to things as I once did. As though I've destroyed the means of cling. Saddens me how it scares some people, people close to me who seem to need me to stay where I've been, in that stuck, that heavy heavy scared place. So I can be managed.

Have the anchorlines snapped? *Sickness needs sickness to hide.* Am I drifting?

All I know is every day I don't get in the woods I feel I've betrayed my own birth. As if I owe my birth a thing, some gratitude. As if I'm talking about creation, talking about God. I am talking about accidents. I am talking about pain and mothers and inheritance and resentment. I am giving birth to another layer. Of soul? Of seeing? Of lungs, a remodeling of body and being? I'm mothering, fathering, childing, but mostly I'm dying and growing and shrinking at the same doggone time. It's not as if I owe it to all the suffering of all things. To breathe this way, among all this. To breathe it in. And give it away. Yes, I owe it to the suffering of all things.

The woods, at least, don't care about me, and suchwise I feel in the woods more cared for than anywhere else.

Here come the leaves again and a breeze as though from another season. But there is only one season anymore.

I was bushwhacking around the other day and stumbled on a big poplar at the edge of the floodplain. The bark seemed to have melted to its present shape. Nubbined and scaled stood that flesh. A riverine mosaic. A stretch and an opening and another gap. I could peel it but it had peeled me first, had left my face, if that, a remnant, some derelict feature in its flank.

I sat near the base of it. Twenty feet up, the tree disappeared in a lake of green. No breeze ruffled that veiny water. It would have taken four of me to hug this poplar, were I the type to hug poplar. Maybe I am, all four of me. Maybe the poplar is a leg and a hug would have tickled it, and it would have lifted me, all fourteen of me, as it stepped back to the Triassic. Big trees seem to be the sky's ambling, the roots of its gait.

In ways, I was fortunate that I couldn't see the top of that tree or even close to the top. Its branches were trees themselves. I have never cut a tree so large, but it must provide a thrill and a sadness like any flirt with death, with slaughter. Hundreds of rings. Each of its burls warted as big as a child's skull and more cratered.

I sat there above the invisible planet of roots. Looking at the tree kept bringing to mind a picture of the moon that I've never seen. The brown, the pale mottlings, had that kind of glow and outerness, a distance though close.

At least it was cool beneath the poplar. At least the birdsong kept putting me back down lightly.

Now the river's a mindfield of beaver or muskrat or big carp slapping the surface as I paddle upstream, trying to get a little speed, trying to ignore the swarm of ants under my canoe's seat and the big spider nesting near the bow. They throttle me up, the bursts of water, five now, six. They appear every several strokes, peace disturbing the peace again.

The air is cool, it's dry, too, and sweet with a smell of mealy apple and other fruits, their skins and pulp. Probably grapes rot under vines on the banks. Probably the ants smell and the river itself. I dip my hand in the water, but against my nose I can only detect remnants of the sandwiches I made for lunch.

What could be better than a lunchbreak canoe jaunt on a good Thursday afternoon? I'm a lucky animal inhabiting a luckier life. Leaves are everywhere on the river like some run come unstitched. A dog barks in the distance, traffic spells tiresounds on the bridge. The breeze pushes the canoe such that I brush a limb with the back of my head. Something drops in the canoe, a grape of nearly perfect roundness and a dark burgundy. Specks like stars dot its plump surface. A green of bleeding leaf is the node where lately it was attached to the vine that hung, laden.

I'm now blown further upstream, but not before shaking a good number of the fruit into the puddle at the bottom of my leaky craft. Bitter but savory are the grapes on tongue, lips, and gums. The skin is thick, gets all up between my teeth. The pulp globular and seedy bursts as if encased in a membrane. This is a gift, another gift in a life of them.

How yellow the river appears where sun filtering through the canopy illuminates it. I want nothing more, but there is more. There is a katydid on my gunwale. It crouches and then hops into flight, a gossamering of wings, kind of awkward but hellbent, too. The shore isn't close, but the bug finds a flood-licked place to land again, a leaf.

And more. The days are more. The heat is more.

I paddle, drift, paddle some more. Two vultures scraggle-winged and dark turn beneath a cloud the color of window trim on a long-abandoned house. They orbit a few times and then are gone. There's a limited space in the sky visible, as trees are a wall on either side of the river where I sit again, letting the breeze blow the canoe where it will.

The jays don't stop their screeching at the deep rumble of the approaching train. The horn blows four times, and it sounds each time more yellow.

A shagbark hickory has fallen here. It lies at a forty-five off the bank. Shoots from a poison ivy vine splay off the flank, everything stripped of leaves and also moppy with other leaves washed to a place bent around vine, twig, branch. Emblems of thicker currents. Scrolled messengers of rain.

There's a spider with a legspan the size of my hand walking up a jewelweed plant on the bank. Alternately it caresses the leaves and flowers as though terrified of its steps. It could be waiting for a bird. How bilious beauty can be. There's a hummingbird. I hear it before or if ever I see it, that sound as if air in love with wings.

The spider trips some wire in me. It must be six feet away as the mosquito flies. What could eat such a form? Only hate knows the angles of those joints, the heat of that abdomen. Hate is witty, a nit, and it'd take an umbrella of a web to hold and feed such a spider. Therefore it stalks, I guess. No wasted flesh. No need for color, for camouflage, for singing, spider is the adamant. It makes new endings. It sees with its motions all darkness to shame.

It's going to rain. The clouds have that thickness thing going on and the river keeps spitting bubbles as though from its silt, as though the body beneath the body of the bottom is breathing hard, puddling with sweat.

August is an intensity, a thickness like abandon. It grips the jugular, climbs it. It buries me in layers that I delight in the taste of even as they bury me with insensate longings.

For instance, how lost is home. How seeing is hearing, as being is, for instance. How a word can be kneaded, a word for all senses firing at once—*oversense, th(o)roughsense*—no stillness but in the trying. For instance, the soft frill of the lobelia blossoms, that scarlet so vibrant the shadows are a nectar.

Storms dumped enough rain overnight for the river to crest its bluff. Ten-foot bluffs. I look at one matted with leaf. Trod and silted, a kind of windblown look. In water normally still I drift downstream among puckering lines of eddy, crease, dimple. The river is carrying some tropical storm oceanward again. Flow breaks against logs just under the surface, breaks with blooming dimples, each ripple from the get-go doomed.

High water is high water. The storms come. What's amazing is the aroma of the land drying out again. Damp mud, damp leaves, damp wood. Isn't a sweet smell, isn't sour either.

It is rich, dirty, the kind of odor I could smear on my body and feel clean again. Smells like a pelt, like blood musky and dense. A smell that was sharp an hour ago before the sun used it to carve a new face on pretty much every log and bank. A smell that creates this day I'll remember years from now. Somewhere I've been already, too placental and utter all over again. The fish feed anyway. And the frogs begin their questions—*are? are? are?*—never to finish them.

So the world spills its guts and gets bashful about it the following day. The hazards of the confessional are many.

An odor of evaporation, of receding. The kind of damp, ribald, cuckoldous indulgence that conjures another thunderstorm just as the bark's about to dry out. A fish rises towards a spider. It pauses, strikes, recedes. Something in my nose itches at the sight of it. The water has a name for it, but only the mushrooms know what it is.

September
Slopes

The canopy, though it shrinks, grows livelier each day. The river couldn't care less, swollen as it is. The river takes the leaves, floats them, swallows them, returns them to silt.

No doubt the river senses a hurricane is on the way, feels it through connections underground, perhaps at its mouth where fish enter and exit like atoms in that tidal breathing.

All I know is the jewelweed is so puckered that it quivers— the blossoms, the stems—in no apparent wind. Seeing them, the winds in me start to turn, they turn harder and faster, demolishing the more useless architecture there. They are funny hats, anyway, the jewelweed blossoms, especially the one fallen orifice-down on a drifting leaf, a little curl of orange, red-splotched and cream-licked at its top.

Mineral knowledge was never my goal, but I am somehow more sifted, more particle, *particle*. No longer do I question it, this simple act—thirty minutes, an hour—of being here, loving what comes, is, each day, or if not every day, as many days as can be mustered. Nothing's quiet now, and I'm okay, okay with this, needing this. These jaunts, these woods.

I walk. I stop. I walk again. And then there's a den, a wet and rocky one. Water trickles with a sound like whispering underwater. The granite drools a softer pink where the stream licks it. Moss clings like an old shag rug. There are chestnut oak leaves. Cliffs jut sharp and bloody with mineral seep, muted golds, violets, greens. An entrance as though to a cave leads to a deadend of darker rock. There's a rusty nail, a twenty penny, wedged in a crevice. There's blacked-over spraypaint, too.

Laurel and spicebush tremble in the seep's own breeze. It breathes, the mountain, the plants, the stone. It all breathes. I breathe as well, yes, and easier than I have in many lifetimes. There's a feather in leaves pressed by the recent rains. Below, a sourwood tree makes a few turns with its trunk, though much slower than that. If there's a name for that motion, it moves at another pace entirely, beyond syllables, where words congeal into soil, some trespasser of dimensions.

This is my seeing listening to what comes in my nose and how my tongue responds to that and responds, too, to the light and dark and the other flutterings of and on my flesh. In the Piedmont, right now this minute (that one), it feels possible to plumb the world as it was, was (will again be) without form, and void.

The rocks ooze. Shadows stir the oozing. I see no footprints. The rocks appear wooden now, their bark granular, ant-deliberate. There are too many spiders to count.

I look for a petroglyph, seems a likely place for one. Lichen and moss are cave art. And cave art, too, the cakes of the mud dauber, the bracken, the galax, the broad beech fern.

What absence will fill the eye next?

Hard rains, the woods an orgy of damp. The ground, the air, everything is spongy and thick. All flux are the rivers. Cliffs drip, ditches turn to creeks, creeks to torrents. I can't sit in the woods without wetting the seat of my pants. It's perfect.

Here a centipede bends and courses through a sphagnum nub, Japan grass, yellowroot, and bracken towering, a little saggy, over it. Hiss of the catbird, the jays out of tune. There is a branch here, a small one and delicate, maybe twelve inches long, about the width of a pencil. A fern clings to the branch, its rust-colored mycelial threads like sticky toes. The branch must have fallen in the spring because buds reach from its ends. There are five white mushrooms growing at the branch's butt. They are delicate, translucent, with veiny lamellae, or gills, the varicosity visible on the cap. The stems could be burnt matches, black at the base as they are. The mushrooms smell like rain, and I'm about to pinch one between lip and gum just as a cloud moves, allowing sunlight to flood the thick grove of fern just uphill.

There's a gulch up there; across it, fallen, several logs damp and half-clothed in mossy bark. Beech, sourwood, and hickory compose the canopy. No mist is visible, but I smell its presence all the same.

There is a day, a September day, the questions come. They fall through me like the rain. How long for the orb weaver to spin a web? Does the web survive a hard rain? What eats the snakeskin? What eats the crow? Will the days, as they grow shorter, suckle the world with different lips? Could the bird (killer) be dissuaded by a certain pattern on the bug's (victim) back or face? How many colors does the leopard frog see? Does stone breathe? Would the air leap if it had legs? Does it have legs? Hasn't it leapt all its life?

I'm walking upstream. To focus on one thing is useless. I'm swept on a flood of interrogation. Will the adelgids kill all the hemlocks? Of what use, medicinally, is poison ivy? When did the river's course turn eastward here? What kind of stone was this before it metamorphosed? If I walk in the woods every day, will the woods walk in me? Is it three o'clock yet? At how many speeds do things rot? Who said, Water that is too pure contains no fish? What color is lightning's blood? What would happen if I didn't drink from the river?

The nettle flowers are fuzzy nodes, a sequence of them on a tough stem. They are silt-caked where the plants grow close to the river, rooted in the mud-faced flank of the bluff.

Rain spreads its blankets on the river. After a few false starts, the falling is steady, the drops small. Upstream there's goldenrod; it seems to be aflame. My eyes fondle it or maybe they fondle its contrast with September's sallow copper.

I could say the sky is a wet sock and put it on and then put on some boots and dance a while, maybe with nothing, maybe for nothing, but hopefully for everyone anywhere in a hard place. This is a month for dancing, for wading thigh-deep in the limp pokeweed, berry-juice staining my slacks. Do I wear slacks? If I wear nothing, do I still wear slacks?

Winter seems far away, but it isn't. Summer seems close, but isn't it? What is the root of rapture? Go on, it's the syca-mores that turn the clocks back, but it is the vines that turn the clocks at all.

I'm drifting in the old canoe again. I'm looking at the sky. There appear to be two layers of cloud. The lower layer trucks north as if on a superhighway of wind. It doesn't seem much higher than a good-sized Appalachian peak, but in the Piedmont, great height is hard to gauge. So few things attain a decent elevation that comparison is impossible.

The upper layer of cloud is wispier than the lower, which is billowy. It might seem the contrary since the upper layer appears stationary. Distance could make the upper layer only appear sta-tionary; it is probably hauling ass.

Appearances matter more than facts where the sky is con-cerned. Anyway, facts are appearances. The fact is this: another tropical storm is centered not far to the west. The edges of it are right above me, heavy in the head and soon on the skin, if not now.

A canoe is not the kind of craft for a fact-hungry traveler. I poke about and drift, notice that in places the river is virtually covered in leaves. High winds have hastened the hackberry's undressing. Things are yellow. Things are green. The water, clear again after several days without rain, reveals logs and sticks, and I draw or sweep with the paddle, sliding the old fiberglass cruiser out of their way.

A new bloom is out, four or five thick white nodes at the head of a three-foot stem rooted in silt collected on an old log. There is lichen like a limestone cliff layered and pale brown near what was once the top of that former tree. An orange pointillism of jewelweed freckles the bank's green, weedy face. Katydids strum their reels, or are those locusts? Always the crickets, their undulant whirring.

I try to locate fruit on the paw paw tree rooted just up the bank, but there doesn't appear to be any fruit. Here the bluffs are too steep and damp and tall for me to park the canoe and walk. Anyway, the paw paw fruit won't be ripe yet. It hasn't been cold.

Crazy how the world wakes from its summer slumber. As though change requires wakefulness, as though a period of dizzying activity is necessary before winter's big sleep.

Suddenly a tree falls with a crack and then a thump. It's too far within the woods to see, but the blue in the sky is the blue of singing, only visible in shifting patches and sometimes not at all.

The river breathes mist. I can see its breath. It smells sweet. It is lavender. It dervishes orangeblue above the orangebrown water. With distance the river turns green. The logs that jut from the bed, not wide logs, appear to be moving. The water, too, seems to move. It does move, but its breath moves more.

If an old soul with mist for a beard and a round hard belly comes now poling out of the mist on an old bamboo junk, smelling like the Ya, that upper tributary of the Yangtze, I'll nod as though no biggie. It's one of those days.

A lot happens in September. The canopy grows skinnier and maybe the sky becomes a yolk endlessly breaking. There goes a squirrel, its leap the loveliest bridge. I never know what the lichen is doing, but it looks busy, especially on the birch limb fallen and snagged twenty feet up the boxelder.

Geese chuckle as they fly overhead. I hear three steamy rasps of a hawk. The birds are more active with their singing than they've been in a long time.

It's rush hour for the seven-thirty work crowd, too. Trucks and vans cross the bridge with the barium whine of retreads on the crosshatch concrete, and I can see the ladders in stacks like dorsal fins.

The mist intoxicates with a dirty purity. I want to be so smoked. I want to be gutted and filleted and then left for a while in smoke of hickory, smoke of dead weeds, the ones with the flowers gone to quiet, brazen seed.

If a lot is happening in September, it is happening. I sit in a place in the sun on a bluff ragged with scrub oak. The viburnum leaves are raspberrying. Green exists, but it's minimal compared to the pink. Along the edges, the leaves are finely toothed. As I run my finger along that texture, I feel the teeth of many fish.

The breeze is solid, steady. Feels thick, feels still.

There are rocks by the thousands among the boulders, more of them than trees. It's like a giant scraped the hill's north side, bleeds white-shaley and pink, glows like feldspar.

Where is my body? It is more foreign now, the future stone of me, the soil. Matter doesn't matter and then it does. More foreign and more me at once the body feels now, as though most at home in outer, scaped.

Sourwood, for instance, at the base of a scree slope cherty and fingerable. Touch it. Drop it. Climb. The river isn't far, always within hearing, closer than earshot.

And where is my worry? Where is that acute sense of constantly letting someone down? Where? Stone flows, too, and slower than glacier. At the pace of becoming nothing again, the truest job, being demolished.

Not that the river is easier or even more comfortable or close. The wind picks up again. Rattle of leaves. Limbs rub. The moment is spark, a fly on a twig in the moss near the eyebrow of the mother of God.

The sun is more on my shoulder now than on my face. I have fallen a hundred times without moving from this rock. Nothing smells like Gore-Tex anymore. My legs are hardly even sore.

Here's a yellowjacket, always they are busy in early fall. The winged thing is all business, all hunger and feeding on a gnawed and curled laurel leaf.

The days go on. They burn. They smolder and blaze. They say, none of this is about you. As the river sheds its skin, it grows another. Smells like snake. Leaves blanket it, small ones, many still green. Hackberry, maple, sweetgum, birch. Galled and mottled, the leaves drift in the dry heat in and out of shade. Bubbles at their edges give the sun back in dots of brilliance like mercury. The leaves with curled, erect nodes catch the breeze and travel more quickly than the others, though with no more purpose.

Some of the leaves sink. They all sink eventually, or else they snag on fallen, silted timbers and sink then even slower. Boxelder, poplar, witch hazel, cherry, shapes as numerous and varied as forms of shine contained by shadows. The sun penetrates, illuminating roots under the surface, a webwork of them near the bank, near the bottom.

Just as the sun has many tongues, a river has many bottoms. I sink into them when I stand here and know that the bottoms are each a surface, that dimension defies description.

The world is voodoo, the kind I need. The river is low again, but it flows through the trees. All the holes conflue. Leaves, too, are cold-blooded. When they shed, they shed to vein. Look at the nettles, their flood-muddied stems, so many holes but none in the veins.

Last day of September, and I sit by the creek listening to the sun spell orange for the rocks underwater. Change swims in the liquidambar. The air is a slow fuse joining the minutes, leaves as sparks, smells as haze. Nothing is native anymore, or else everything. The dogwood learns the architecture of peach through color more than taste. It grows foreign to itself. The slope where it roots holds it as it holds the slope. The Japan grass is what I get when I divide abundance by swarm. Things live, but mostly things shrink with a kind of inward swelling, they wrinkle and bleed.

I hold a rock in order that it holds me, hostage to its puny caves. Everyone knows that in the minute dwells the everlasting, but whoever said it is more summer than fall if we ignore inertia and live by sight alone, the most fascist of senses, that joker needs a job. I want to believe that quartz is September's state stone, it has Piedmont all over it anyway.

The clouds are just a bunch of leaves falling from weather's tree. They never land, but they come close. Wind landscapes. Water is just wind with more faith and cheaper by the hour. September is verve; it imps summer's broken wings. I know this today because it is tomorrow too soon and with it October, or just another name change.

White lichen is as paint on the boulder midstream, moss is as stain. Could be the minutes are stiller than loving well—ask the spiders, no, lick their young.

Meanwhile water orbits water. Silk is a mist. The beech trees stand like so many femurs on the bank. The flattest place speaks best of the steeps. I breathe an air cooling to a lemon no time zone can contain. As usual, the sun is a juicer. It pulps.

October
Interiors

Life is a slower falling. And soon, such as gravity is, it is a rising. Sooner or later everything is edible. October, and I fall through the surfaces. I rise underneath. There's a stick with life's face on it rendered in lichen and warts.

The creek breaks into four channels as it runs over a boulder. Sunlight makes popcorn on two of the channels, and the wind butters it. The air smells of fern, wet leaves, and wild ginger. It smells of creek and stone, lichen on wood.

Mushrooms rot, dark masses on the ground as though something melted there. Could be deer puke, could be. I cross boulders, duck under limbs. The air is crisp and burned with a coolness like salt. In places the sky is visible over the river, a sky the color of kneeling. I do not kneel now. I touch the river; it shakes my hand, letting go its only grip.

The pressure of roots. *Kneadful.* The land a network of bridges, a web. Anything with legs is, in essence, a spider, except in the desert, maybe, where there are few trees, few roots. How could the soil feel so abstract, so temporary when it is a hardness of fodder, when it is a sky only more dense?

There's a gouge in the beech tree as though its bark has ripped, as if stretchmarks. Maybe this was a good summer for growth. All its leaves are green. Most of the canopy is green and wind-chopped. Bugs sail on that body.

It's the canopy underfoot that brasses and burgundies, so much gold and purple blood, summer's postscript. There could be a hundred turtles just under the ground here. The earth is so humped, so sphagnum, so legged, so moving. I sense that it's all a suspension, a bridge to another bridge and thereforth and go on. The heights are greater than I know and that is lucky, for I walk more recklessly these days, sit, even sprawl with little regard for falling through to the other side and maybe farther, maybe not.

Another October day, crisp and bright and cloudless. The reflection on the river of trees slowly goldening, of the quarried cliff's scar, of a blue so opaque with shine the bottom of the river leaps from it. These reflections set my marrow to flowing. This is the fourth step towards nowhere. The first three steps are written on the leaves drifting by, but who can say on which leaves has attained that stillness and is too much with us to say.

Air is blood and the world vamps, sucking it anyway it can. The island sinks so it can grow, a choke, a clog. Along its edges, the water drinks, spits.

Meanwhile, two birds flit in a dogwood, the leaves a slow bleeding. They squeak, the birds, they are small and nearly hidden.

The canoe slides on. There's an island of bent Joe Pye weed and sand, a coarse mixture of sand, the grains like seeds speckled rose, cream, brown, white, blue. Like the buds of tiny flowers on dwarf if not invisible stalks.

I let the sand fall through my fingers and listen as it rubs, grinds with a sensual scratching. Nothing is ever clean. No island is always an island; the silted leaves are a testament.

Friction does not argue. It is a principle, a law, unchanging yet variable according to forces, meaning it means too much to mean or not mean. Besides, the water leaves the sand here; a certain wrinkle in the flow makes it thus.

Elsewhere the island is mud. Elsewhere there are weeds ragged and tragically hued with late green's wild moods. The weeds hold the island together. The island holds them and each holds itself accordingly.

Splayed shells, freshwater clams open and white like eyes that need no fire, no nerves, no face. Maybe they aren't sightless. Maybe they see the memory of their late flesh, the mouths that stole that flesh, the teeth or fingers that opened them like this.

The weather is clear for many days. I miss the rain. The river is so clear now and slow. It seems as though the leaves could overwhelm it, falling as they are at a steadier pace. My eyes almost grow used to the brightness each day. The heavier dew and the cold mornings drive wedges in my hardest stumps. Morning walks mean drenched shoes and socks, mean cold fingers, too.

There are many river oats growing. They bend with the weight of seed. The pods are like basketry, like feathers. There are seven to nine of the flat, segmented growths on each stalk. The light reflected off the river makes a similar crosshatched pattern on pretty much everything, the bottoms of leaves, limbs, trunks. All of it bounces and sways in the breeze.

Downstream, the river bends to the left. A creek enters just before the outside of the bend, water in it gurgling over and through sticks of a beaver lodge. There's a lot of orange in the water, especially at the boundary of shadow and light. One mosaic on top of another is the surface, the layers of limbs and foliage, the sky, the ripples, the various contortions of darkness and its inverse.

All over the places I regularly wander there are new vistas. Some days the places themselves appear new. Even now I look at the river again and see the rocks at the bottom, small ones the size of a hand and several larger, though none too large to fit in an oven. They resemble bread in color and shape. Like bread, they have been kneaded and baked.

My canoe's bow slides onto a sandspit that's almost covered with leaves. Something delightfully raw about fallen beech leaves; the fact that so many hang on and for so long might have a little to do with it. A beaver-gnawed branch lies in the shallows here, and its pointed end, toothmarked, looks downright tasty. The color of the wet wood is as thrilling as the border where the stripped wood meets the bark with an abrupt answering of every question never asked.

The sky says kiss a beaver to discover such questions. Says a kiss is the ultimate in information technology. If the world is a web, why not be wide on it, spiders with no limit to domain. But no high speed, not now. In autumn, the world says give me back, enough chlorophyll, I need it quieter, stiller, colder, slower, pared to the bones.

Transition is the rule in the Piedmont, sprawled and inhabited as it is between the Appalachian foothills and the Coastal Plain. The water passes through. Fewer watersheds have their sources here than in the mountains. Large vistas, peaks, and expansive water are not common. In terms of oceanward flow, the transport of nutrients and the collection of them—erosion, silting—the Piedmont is the middle ground. If the mountains collect, provide, and the coast dumps, then the Piedmont delivers.

I watch a polypody fern hang on the cutbank. Though it's still, it is busy—the green says so. There are seven thousand faces in the mud of the bank and none of them are human, though many look that way. There are new species previewed in the strata and extinct ones, too. Smilax, manic conduit, roots in the berm above the ferns. The spines are green at the base, then yellow, then a heavy umber as though stained with blood, but not.

Very few folks, when asked the meaning of life, will point to the smilax. That is a shame. The plant is the heart of so many banks, its roots a kind of fixed parachute and gravity both.

Once I saw spartina in a marsh near the edge of the continent. It had the same color pattern as the smilax's spines—green, yellow, red. The tides did that, the exposure to salt and air and flow. The ocean that was once here, in the Piedmont, remains in spirit. The siltstains, the gnatswarm midstream, that dissertation on dizziness. Somewhere, maybe in the stickpile near the box-elder, a frog croaks in time with it. Out here even the soloists accompany everything.

The senses are memory, and I remember through their vast catalog of impressions. And maybe memory is the mulch of spirit. I cannot see anything now. It is Saturday. One breath, the next, and the canoe has drifted into a place where sunlight pops and sizzles off the water with glorious vengeance. I see nothing and more. The senses are a deeper woods, always close, always primitive.

There was a time in my childhood, I don't remember the day or year, when I knew that my senses were the only thinking I was ever going to trust. Only now am I coming to terms with this.

Turning from the light, I see a small spiderweb strung between the leaves of a river oat brown and wilted and hanging over the river as though it leapt but tangled in its own falling. A little spider stands in the middle; it could have quite a time on my thumbnail, it is so small.

Midstream, many leaves travel solo. The sun glows bluer and streaked. Birdsong is muffled and fidgety both. I'm filled with buttery, mealy, fermenting smells as of evaporation and rot and mud. The birds crank all at once with their various noises. I cannot see them, but they are flying, they are landing and hopping on my tongue, cleaning my teeth and then my brain with squarks and rattles and cheeps.

The sun makes a white plank on the river under a walnut tree all but stripped of leaf. Only the lowest and apparently newer branches hold substantial foliage. There the leaves are green near the center and brown on the edges. They remind me of a spider's abdomen. So many spiders have striped coloring like this, though not always green and brown.

Mist slides in swarms of feathering and curl. I don't see it unless the sun shows it to me and I happen to look. Who can say why or at what and by what forces we happen to look? Talking about grace, the mist inside, and the sun, and how much I must not see because I look.

Among October's diminishments I continue to wander. The days are shorter, the trees barer and larger-appearing. Fewer insects patrol the air. It's dark at seven and dark again at seven. The dwindling soothes, it just does.

The cycle of seasons is always more dramatic at the cusps, when summer bleeds to fall, fall descends to winter, winter births spring, which soon erupts in summer. Every year is a new generation, always different, always the same. The straightaways of deep summer do not lack drama, but things get pretty crazy and quickly in October, just as they do in March, in June, and in December.

It is largely textural, how I sense the changes. Maybe it is only through texture, the depths of the surface. The sounds, too, are different. One morning, for instance, there are so many crowsounds. Traffic-noise permeates the thinning canopy from farther away. I spook a pair of wood ducks instead of the heron I've seen for much of the summer. Leaves snag on the canoe's bow and throw water in a glorious fan as the boat moves forward. Leaves ricochet off leaves as they fall, whispering something, maybe recipes for a decent life. The thick, grey days foretell snow rather than remnants of tropical storm. My body shifts, too. I eat differently. I want to sleep more. I grow more interested in the house, in pointing the bricks, cleaning and capping the chimney, gathering wood, getting down in the crawlspace.

I'm beginning to walk with no spiderwebs in my hair. There's a sour, fermented smell to the air. Seed and fruit replace pollen and blossoms as the season's gestures of choice. I want to make love in the mornings. I want to hold my love longer after doing so. The distance between us ripens sensually. Sap stays closer to home.

But still I take these jaunts. The river, the woods, the critters, the seeing and not seeing. I need the space, need that gnat, a fuzzy one, drifting on the air. Now it lands on a leaf of a nettle rooted on a log half underwater. The gnat crawls under the leaf, drawing my eye to the silty mess of brown leaf and slow rot that dangles there. The insect flies again. Or it levitates. It could be a ball of flowerstuff, a winged seed; maybe that's its camouflage or its origin. The gnat flies close to my face now. I'm surprised by its long legs. Will a bug like that survive the Piedmont winter?

Some days the world feels like an eyeball and everything on it just motes, little visuals, tracers, life a big migraine the sun won't stop tripping out on. If I lived by no calendar, had no numbers or names for the days and months, I'd have to invent them. Flux terrifies. I love flux. I give it a name, "flux," and other words rise like fish to that gnat. "Terror," "love," "spirit," "breath," "go," "thanks." My names for October would change each year, depending on the weather, inner and outer. Friends in other regions, they would certainly have different names for the days and months and seasons and perhaps different numbers, too.

Today, the words for October resemble a crow's call. They smoke off the tongue the way orange oozes greenly from the hackberry at the bend downstream.

The interior is everywhere in October, more apparent with the change of season, more prevalent. Summer is rich in edges, thick with faces and bodies. There's a guarded sense in summer, as though the heavy foliage, the elaborate flowers and webs and insects hide something deeper. This is not so. The depth is here on the surfaces, on all the surfaces, for in summer there was never only one. By depth: the infinite, the voidspirit that exists at the center and orbits the center both. The ultimate interior ever oozing forth and away, other side of the next other side and the nearer side of the closest.

Now there is less mass. Vistas appear. I could not see through the goldenrod a month ago. I could not see the great log six feet beyond the edge of the river. Is there more now? Is there less? There's a shift in mass, at least visually. Depth replaces mass. There is more perspective. I see through the stalks to more stalks and then through them to see through the limbs. So on swells. The eyes adjust but are no more active than in July when I stared at the textures and patterns of the goldenrod's growth.

One can always look up. Being on the river allows in many cases a vista unceilinged by branches. There are clouds, the various languages of blue. I like looking up now and then, as though the sky's unhindered by season. If the woods are a fast forward, the ground the play, then the sky is the pause. The sky is no slower though, no less playful. It makes a different kind of dizzy than the woods.

Another morning, another paddle up the little river. Two turtles plop from logs with a splash. A maple has gone to flare in the last day or two, like it was smoldering, all coals for a while, and then the wind spoke to it, said the right thing.

Jays are foghorns. There is no fog, but there is cloud. The river is clouded, the sky is clouded. There's a boulder in the water near the edge of the river; I've come to using it to gauge the river level. Leaves hurry past the stone. There are faint dimples in the water, creases as if distressed glass. Slick brown silt rings the rock several inches from the riverline.

Another outcrop, probably cousin to the rock in the water, an extrusion of the same vein, stands on the bank. It's garlanded with weeds, a collage of lichen and moss and fallen leaf. Farther in, the bank's interior gets steep quick. Granite lumps speckle the slope. I could be staring at a loaf of rich, multigrain bread torn open. There are so many cavities and nooks, fall's color parade a multitude of fruit and seed milled and milling.

So it goes. When I can, I hop in my boat and paddle. Or I start walking. I watch the water where the woods and the sky mingle, and sometimes I see beneath the reflection. The interior is everywhere, surface or source or not. And so is the source everywhere. I am never lost, but I'm always getting lost. The whole outing might take an hour. I don't think about it the rest of the day. It comes back to me all day. Things I don't know I felt or saw, tasted or heard—they come back, they linger, they go.

The dew seems to thicken with the cooler mornings. It's a sloppy, wet slog through the weeds at the edge of the woods. I wonder if such a buildup of moisture is a prerequisite for first frost. I see little creeks run through the lawns and edgeplaces as I bike to the bridge, off to the side of which my canoe is stashed, less and less camouflaged by foliage. Each night it's as if a lick of atmosphere has descended to form its own system close to the ground.

One morning I sit against a chestnut oak atop the bluff above the floodplain. The river is mist and shimmer, a few streaks of it visible through the growth. There are three large poplars at the foot of the bluff, and I'm looking down, out, and up at various parts of them when something crazy happens. There are all these birds squeaking and fluttering through the limbs. I am soaking up their activity, their song, their agile, need-corniced movements. A trajectory, the sum of their motions like conception or just taking another breath. I am sitting here in my hooded sweatshirt, watching the trees, birds, the patches of sunshine, the wild ginger's milky patterns, when a ruckus of feathers erupts ten feet to my left. There's another big chestnut oak there. What I see is a hawk's fanned tail just as it lifts prone and digs its talons into a songbird mid-flight. They hit the leaves briefly and don't stay there. The hawk takes the little bird—there are so many trees I can't tell what kind of bird—down to the floodplain's floor. All the while the hawk keeps belting an alarming, aggressive call. For a moment the voice seems to belong to the victim, but the vocals last too long.

Twilight, and yellow apple sky at the rim of the powerline cut. Scrub oak a frizzy outline against the horizon. There's a new moon, a sapling blackjack oak. The above contains a star, too, no, two. Things get arthritic this time of day, the sky drained of all but the most distant light. Things constrict. This time of year is the year's evening. Soon will be the dusk days. No more dog days, these. Wood duck days and roadkilled fox. Who can say when there will be frost? October wears me tight. If I'm warm, it is because I burn. Inward is a messier woods. Laughter lives there like gravity, like love, opens me to bugs and crickets, the passing plane. No green as deep as that which the laurel leaves wear now up here on the slopes above the river. And through them the morsels of a sky so purple it ferments, devouring the moon's pale sugar.

To experience the nature of the Piedmont woods, I have to participate. I have to want it, at least a little bit, even if I need it. Either way, it doesn't want me. It doesn't need me. Glorious sights or what are commonly marketed as such—peaks, gorges, rugged cliffs and coasts—are not the reality here. Here, a simple piece of driftwood is never so simple; its every notch, burl, groove extends miraculous.

The eyes are daddy long legs bouncing from one thing to the next. The color and pattern of the river oats against the bank, I drink them. And I swallow the warts on the hackberry. The land is its parts and each part is a sum and part of a sum.

I'm in a grove of laurel. It's a den, with curly, lichen-fuzzy branches like an infinity, a closeness, an imprisonment of wonder, of world. The river traffics almost directly below. A bit more erosion and this would be a cliff more than a slope. The laurel's roots hold and keep hold. There is much green in the nucleus here, green and brown, the evergreen of the laurel's leather tongues, the frosty lime of lichen, and barkbrown. A squirrel with a fat acorn in its jaw skitters loudly through the grove and comes to sit on a branch not three feet from me. Beyond the furry critter it is hard not to watch the parade of yellow leaves on the river. A small river and but a fraction of it visible from here, yet so many leaves.

If I take the narrow, inadequate definition of place as being that which I see, then even this one is neverending. For I see the grey, wet, heavy sky and sourwood leaves like a tarnishment before it. How did I get here? I was headed home from the store. The seeds are everywhere and a tick is crawling on my jeans. A tick in October! I don't know there are so many seeds until the leaves begin to drop. I could try to describe the color of a certain small tree. I could say variegated or tobacco, say color of allergies, of polyp or red snapper (which are always pink and even then of an orangey sort).

The rain approaches more slowly now. Gone are the sprung traps of summer's afternoon boomers and drenchers. The urgent masses of last month's tropical storms are gone, too, somewhere else. Now the sky grows cloudy, grey, dense, and stays that way for a few days, the sun perhaps breaking through here and there. And then the rain falls, if at all, slowly.

The cloudtrees, too, seem to be losing their leaves. The air turns mild. I hope it will rain. The color in the trees is highly charged against the dark sky. The leafshapes are more distinct with the different colors oozing from the different trees. The voracity of hues astonishes, how they maw, hungry wavelengths. In summer the gash of red clay at an overturned tree's base was a shocking contrast to the green flood. Now I hardly notice red clay unless I'm slipping on it or it's one of the impressions I conjure to comprehend the beech leaves' serrations.

Upstream there's a tree so on fire it burns blue. Of course it's red, a deepness of red that suggests purple and yellow both. It isn't the only garish tree of the lot. The hardwoods that retain a solid measure of their summer green are in the minority now. Brassy, copperish hues dominate.

I'm not the only one ripped on October's broth. The squirrels scooch among the branches, cheeks fat with nuts, their entire motion a sublimation of the land. Leaf litter sprawls on the equally littersome shrubs and weeds. Who could doubt permanence amongst such vigorous disappearance? I love how in scraggle and dwindle there is, such is.

November
Roots

November flirts with silence everywhere I look. The leaves slump and cover their ears. Or else the leaves are ears and cover each other. Either way, it's an ear jam, a clog. It inspires quiet, emptying-of-canopy does. Quiet is not silence. Silence is more harsh, more total in its withholding. Either way, space grows, perspective stretches, and sound travels through the spaces, but there is still less sound.

The woods are an orchestra of skeletons. Limbs, the trees' winter language, are so numerous now on the horizon. Slow as the changes October wrought, the barren canopy, if it can be called barren, startles. Or maybe it's the larger sky that surprises. The Piedmont sky shrinks in the warm months, leaves become the sky, the thick canopy a cumulus of greens.

Silence is never accurate. What I hear is clackety, abrasive, raw. Something to do with breathing, the land's, and the changes in that throat. Body is perception, soul is too. The joints ache in November. Blood, like the days, grows thin. The ground is a litter, highly mulched.

As the quiet grows broad, I sit against logs that have known floods, been moved. They make good seats. Often they are smooth, not hard to mistake for stones, but their colors are warmer. One, for instance, is black, brown, and beige. I sit on it and picture latitudes, clouds in hues enmeshed on the breeze, a breeze made by moving water, the water's friction and slip (its yearn) as it encounters stone.

Fewer leaves fall. They can only fall further and become silt. It's slower than falling, closer to integration than falling, veins to silt, silt to mud. I walk the logs to know this. The logs that teeter explain it best. When I fall, I go carefully, letting gravity have every atom.

A stick bobs in the current. More and more, neither here nor there, is nor was. Stick's third is under water, doesn't take much. It is, some conglomeration, and it's perfect. Thrice-forked, this delicate branch, and lichen-mottled, a miniature of the clouds in splotches on the blue. And then a certain stone takes me in its cold fingers. It drags me from colder water and shakes. The stone is greyolive, and its lines suggest that it has recently broken from another stone, that it is a fragment. It wears a poplar leaf that retains a spark in its yellow, a spark that most of the other leaves have subsumed. The rock throws me, it has a good arm, but I do not skip. I boomerang. I orbit the stone. It's lovely, orbiting always was. There are many sticks and logs. The stone has spirit and up and orbits me. I do this a while, careful as I can be among the pointed sticks.

The less said about roots the better. They tempt me still, their stretch and depth and probing. Fallen tree's rootclump speaks of dizziness and tears. Rootclump says, go on, hunker on. The mass of soil and stringy, woody material almost resembles a shrub were it not so sagging. The one on the bank now holds rocks in its cavities; this is not unusual (what is?), yet it reminds me of the grip inherent in growth.

Roots are the cirrus of the sky beneath. Roots are or-bitsource. The fog of topsoil hides their shapes and motions. I wonder if legged bodies, like the tree, grow down and up as well as out, and at what proportions. Probably individuals vary according to gene codes, but the ratios, I suspect, are similar across the species.

Though the vistas expand and there is more sky visible, my thoughts in fall tend earthward. Nothing new. I find myself with a shovel more than with a ladder. Often I'm on my knees. Likewise the shadows dig, seek interiors previously buried by summer's outgoing ways.

Earlier I saw a mink while biking the short way to the river. I was crossing the train tracks, at the edge of an industrial park, when the slender black creature shuffled with marvelous hurry into a ditch between the tracks and the road. Strange place for a mink.

Leaves orbit or else they drift haphazard. *Strange is every place, strange and all its traditions.* Leaves orbiting nothing, leaves orbiting other orbits. The world is so many bodies constantly making whoopee and getting on with it all the same. What will knock my socks off next? What will level me? What will make my eyes never open the same way again, make each new breath even newer with its being?

So many stories, each of endless chapters, each a constant chaptering. This story, the bark writes it in bark with bark, and just as the lines fall apart, the insects keep tunneling through that bark, lichen and moss setting up shop where they will, little stillnesses, tones, clues.

November the eighth and frost for the first time since March. It lies on the land, a thin fur. It gets me moving early. The river is warmer than the air. I walk, propelled by cold toes.

Where I sit is not a choice but a motion closer to falling. There is climbing involved. Galax is busy at the low flank of an outcrop, and it draws me forth with its waxy, thick-veined leaves. For a while I feel scribbled by its presence. A little crazily its scribblings flit and form. I scratch them like so many bug bites.

Frost gets me giddy. It is like some long-awaited visitor I am never sure will arrive. Frost is a kind of faith again, though to sense this requires a measure of its absence.

Beech leaves are prominent on the limbs. In places they are the view. I dance through them by the thousands. They twirl me into a near seizure and I surface before I'm under. I'll never understand, nor overstand, the meaning of sanguine again, though it's the bones of November's stock.

A few maple leaves haven't let go. One branch holds ten or so. They dangle like butterflies anchored to another sort of flying. I'm coming to believe, contrary to knowledge, that the breeze is the trees' breathing, but often I hold the birds responsible.

A checkerback knocks on a rotted trunk. Its silhouette glows a thousand shadows. It flutters its wings. It hops and swings and then puts beak to wood again, and I no longer can see the names of things but I see the things and hear them unsaying every name until their namelessness names me, again: *fool.*

If woods, if their frequencies. If Piedmont, if fertile upland, *mountain-foot.*

If I close my eyes even when my eyes are closed, such that they are opened as from within and under the river's bottoms, the canopy's elevations, the bark's furrowings.

If these Piedmont woods give my blood a kind of sunburn (sunborn), if amplification, if this land is, in essence, a complaint and a rebirth.

This is not protest, this place, not yesterday's either. This is not resentment, not resistance. This is not what's flammable in me or them or anything else. Nor douse, wiggler, nor dowse. This is witness. No, it's not witness. This is making love. No, it's love, making. This is succession, a soiling.

Yes, this is not walking around in the woods. This is witnessing's footprints. This is the woods walking around in the woods and a guy trying to catch a glimpse. This is not (definitely not) nature loving me calling nature my bitch. To follow without trying to, this is Piedmont's essence. *This*, and to know etymologies of every common name, the catches in the breath, the releases.

Fused themselves, motion and sound fuse color with feeling. The world a torch in the hands of a mad welder come lately to the craft. There are no Band-Aids, thank goodness, solvent enough for such bleeding.

November means exposure. The river drops, displaying sandbars and edges and stones that were buried by hurricane season, or if not buried, simply existing in a wetter world than this, wetter but no more fluid. The big hill they call a mountain is streaky too. From the canoe, I see its interior flanks, the cliffs and gulches and groves. Trails appear as thin, worn lines in the leaves. I pull the canoe over at a break in the bank's steeps and discover flotsam previously buried in the foliage of alder, yellowroot, and boxelder, the latter strung with samaras. I know less and less each day, about why I'm here, how I got here, what and who drives me, but the intimacy of exposure is always blowing my mind, bringing me closer to the distances that make proximity and, henceforth, dying possible. I paddle the canoe in circles. I pick up rocks thinking they are arrowheads and find they are balls of mud. The deer that's barking grows me a tail. Only a crow fluttering its wings against a cloud-thin sky brings me down to earth. It's like waking from a nap I didn't intend to have in a place I never knew I wanted to be. And there is a beech leaf on my cheek and so many on the rest of my body that I am warm as though in the quilt of another body.

Even so, more animals are dead now. I see them on the streets: possum, coon, deer, cat, dog. Their smells travel delicately on the cold air. Summer was a forgery, brilliant and fun, though a little long in the staying. Fall isn't about death, not melancholy either. And less exposure than a kind of bearing, a giddy distilling and dance of skins.

Each day, the woods have just been born. It won't be the last time either. How many rattles can the land possess? There are many answers everywhere unattainable, just waiting for the proper dismay. It is windy and all the dead have never been so alive. And that's the thing about love; this is where it leaves me after stealing my white flags.

The rocks crumble like voices. I begin to scale a boulder and drag a piece from its side. November cultures the land's milk. Opposites unite. Shrinkage allows expansion. Just try to hide. The sky's lips purse before smiling. Then they open and gnaw on me with puppy teeth. It's a matter of suspension. An illusion of matter. The poplar tree was always a river, only the leaves drained it for a while. Those little goblets on its limbs raise a toast now—to fishsmells of damp leaves, to lines the eyes ride— log rot, the shadows' shafts, spaces between the laurel leaves. To the way things go canary and later fires kindle.

I walk only to discover a floating world in which I'm carried, dragged, and then harnessed to pull. Old mushrooms like balls of spidersilk. And the sky chewing and swallowing beyond all examination or even taste.

Rain falls. Maybe the land summons it. *Yes and no, the unfixing.* Maybe it runs from the clouds or maybe it's been banished, late, late rent. I find a small gulch where an outcrop provides dry harbor. Though the day is apparently windless, breath hurries behind me, wafts under the rocks and then out. The world loud with patter and slap. Leaves bound and limbs tremble. This is not drizzle.

I wonder how long the rain travels before meeting the land—seconds, minutes—and if it breaks as it falls, does it separate into equal sizes? I like to watch the rain conform to its surroundings even as the surroundings transform with it. Hardly three seconds pass without a drop landing on a stone shelf the size of a book. Moss wears the stone, absorbs the moisture.

Pools form in many of the leaves scattered and bent and torn on the stone and dirt slope. What was a crinkly, delicate strata is now limp smudge. Color deepens—these are mostly beech and oak leaves—to a brown more red than brown. Earlier these leaves tended toward yellow. Even now they resist being pinned to a single place in the spectrum. Purity belongs to another season, although the laurel leaves are always close to pure green. In various lights, however, I've called them purple. As usual, words fall short. Like rain, the paths and distances of falling short are worth a little time and sometimes more.

Today—and many other days—the words are rain born in vision's clouds. But vision is ignorance, and the words fall where they will, bouncing down the mind's leafladder. Woods. Or words. In fall, the mind bears a changing canopy too. It is as though foliage was a ceiling and now it has fallen to the ground.

The trees' details—bark, burls, hollows—are hard to see in the mist, which is rot-aromaed and bears a heavy sweetness. My lungs feel lined with fine silt. And still the trees more than ever appear present. They appear to be part of the sky. There is no border. The rain brings everything together in a soggy, sensual commons.

And sometimes the rain stops, little lenses, little eyes variously irised.

The milky, mineral-stained granite is a quilt on which my clothing is another and as patchworked. The moss fuzzy and tubered like some coral leftover from a sea long receded. It isn't chance that stops me here, it is chance's zany aunt. I've lost her name.

I sit on an exposed flank. There are trees and fields and buildings. It isn't so busy. The sky is heavy, a copper and blue, cream-streaked and softly aglow, a low stucco ceiling sagging as though from years under a leaky roof.

Scrub pines frame the view. They are of uninspired height, but the way they sway in the wind, the limbs anyway, is worth much coin. Their cones are small, the largest not much more than a golfball in size. And how abundantly they appear, twenty or more per branch, the branches nonuniform in terms of their growth angles. They are sloppy, disheveled trees, creatures of exposure, weather-weary, battered. They're birdshit-stained and sap sloppy. But as if from that ooze, they exude an aura of persistence. It isn't hard to see them as nearly dead as they are deadly alive.

And now for heaven's sake the nuthatches invade. Their song is like so many phones left off the hook, though creamier. They bounce and flit from one place to the next, heads so ying-yanged and quick on the neck. They remind me of lumps in a snake's gullet. A black snake, to be specific. They look so gullible and delicious, easy prey for felines and other lovers of meat that know air, flight.

It is decidedly evergreen on this thumb of the flank. Laurel, moss, lichen, pine. Fall grows slower and more stubbornly each day. Perhaps it's the mild air, the rain at night smudging leaf colors into deeper degrees of shine. Fall in the Piedmont flirts with winter the way spring plays with summer. The transition is slow and sometimes frenetic. Just when I think it's winter, my body fills with the brisk emptiness, and the leaves seem to last forever.

Another day, and I sit by the creek, watch its slate brown waters rise. Even if they fall, they rise. Fog lifts, slow as fog when the rain still falls and the sun hasn't broken through the clouds. There is rain.

Rain and spleenwort. Rain and yellowroot gone mustard. On beech and chestnut oak, on laurel and limb. And densely in the moss, the clouds a hatchery. Nothing dry, not one thing underneath the other side of darkness there parabalaed between believing's spheres. Only the plural of it and in a breeze the displacement of falling olive and brown. Drabber smears of rain. Particulate almost. Rain squared and the round root of each grey bubble unverbed for a while, little warps, little returnings.

The bank is steep here. Yellow Japan grass, honeysuckle, and leaves smear together on it. A place of dangle and slide. A sapling red oak is as an umbrella growing slightly lower than horizontal, its leaves crimson at the veins and brownish pumpkin without. Six growths stem from the roots. There is nothing desperate in its bearing, nothing emotional at all.

A crow lands on the point of a big dead oak and begins to imitate its mama. Earlier a catbird hissed, feathering my bones. There's a beech tree fallen parallel with the tree where I sit, and its roots are so entangled with this one's roots that the two trees seem to have toppled together. But the beech is still alive, its leaf-bearing branches emergent from its edges' upper sides.

The creek is thirty feet wide and cutbanked, its banks rising two to ten feet before the floodplain. Though I sit on a rot-soft log, the creek carries me. I'm carried, and what else is new. In these parts, many creeks are named for churches. But it is the rain that baptizes me. It is always the rain, whether the rain is falling or moving in the river, the clouds, the blood, the ground.

Strange to still find spiderwebs in the woods. I see a grasshopper, too; it feels me first and part hops, part flies to a sapling beech limb. It is more brown than good maple syrup. I never knew that grasshoppers lived nearly to December. Probably their life spans vary according to the season's whims.

I sit on a log beside a lusty seep that patters and slaps down a boulder's face. The land feels more exposed to me than ever. It doesn't seem barren but appears wide open, as though its thickness and essence shifts inward and downward with the falling of the leaves and the containment of growth processes.

The falling water soothes. The breaking water soothes even more, its music drowning the trafficsounds from roads nearby. Roads are always nearby. There is usually traffic on the roads and in the woods.

Water drips down the moss-shaggy cliff, over and through beech and chestnut oak leaves pasted there, the motions barely audible through the more consistent splattering of the flume beside me. The energy and form of the heavy flow resembles a tongue, as if the cliff has some kind of mouth and throat and is thirsty. I offer it my breath, and what happens next is nothing, as usual, and everything.

That flank of the hill rings with pigments of many lands and times. Many selves, continuous and changing. I like how the colors, what I perceive them to be, are not the colors. That every color I see is a reject, the one wavelength of light that the stone or the lichen or moss on it does not absorb. Am I, too, what I cannot absorb?

Echos of gravity, echos of light. November reeks of traveling aromas, smells that escort me further into the present and the past and future all at once. Like most things, perhaps, I spill what I absorb and shine with what I do not. Time is always sensual, many sensations converging, diverging, fading, flaring. I look at the tree before the next tree, doesn't matter what kind, and know that I've been dead longer than I've been alive. Yes, autumn guts me as sure as any roadkilled red fox. The rain makes a soup of light out of those bones. I don't know what feeds on it now, and such ignorance nourishes, some cosmic nut butter.

Speaking of mast, I don't see one acorn or even a husk of any fruit or nut. There are many leaves on the ground. *As many grounds in the plasma.* There's an aerial view of a boreal forest in miniature on a chunk of granitic quartz. The lichen resembles cliffs and boulders. There are hawthorns and highbush blueberry in the mix. A seed could be a chestnut-sided warbler. Nothing is horizontal anyway.

December
Origins

Winter means digestion. All summer's grazing, the slow chewing of fall, has moved to the year's stomach. Cold and wet begin to work on the matter—leaf, wood, crap, dead animals, dead bugs. It's not rot so much as nourishment. The world may appear leanest in winter, but deep down, in belly and soul, it fattens. I listen carefully—wind rattle, tumble of stone, thaw—to hear such changes. Or not at all.

I ride the old bike to the river. Mist is the river's frost, another surface, and how much it moves and how much river is moving under it is of no consequence.

How quickly the day-lingering moon calls the mist to roost, the three-quarter waning moon floating like a boletus on the river and its reflection. The day is not about reality. The woods, the colors of the woods, the river, the cold ache towards numbness in the fingers, none of it, being so real, is about reality.

Now the mist rolls its blankets. Looking upstream I see stretches of the greylavender and they're interspersed by the clean, mistless, water-perturbed water.

On the weeds and leaves the sparkle drains from the frost. Wet is nearly wet again. I have no name for the gods, but I know they are plural now. The banks seem petrified in silt, the river oats especially, they are so still. Something is green and thankfully I do not know its name.

There's a bird now, a flicker, cooing, feet on vine, eating poison ivy berries. The flicker is a large bird, and this one backlit, but I see the red streak on the rear of its neck. It's twenty feet above the river, which now shines green at its depths and saffron at the sandy shallows. A pair of blackbirds streaks a banking, parabolaed path to the other bank. Below the cirrus, those stretchmarks on a lapis flesh, a buzzard soars. The flicker shifts footing and the vines turn it nearly upside down.

The bird doesn't stay long. With a couple of wingbeats it lands on a maple's trunk and pecks a few times. Now a handful of chickadees lands in the scraggle of vines above where the flicker fed. They grow noisier, as though pleased with the eating or saying *keep away this is my grub.*

There couldn't be much pulp left in those berries. But the flesh and the meal, desiccated as it is, is something. Who knows what a bird tastes? Their digestive juices have to be miraculous.

It is probably forty degrees. I've always liked this temperature, especially when it is raining. Everything in sight seems fodder for pigment. Perhaps light at the frequency of green inspires a more lusty reverence.

For a while I watch sunlight skitter on the river's surface like so many fast bugs enflamed with shine. Open mollusks lie in the sand. They hold sand in their pale purple hollows. There's nothing like dying to stay alive, and all the trees fallen in the river say so even more wildly and with size and tangle. The bleached mollusk shells resemble heron crap in size and layout. Random was never random in the end. And from the beginning either.

December is duskclose and very violet. Nothing is singular, or if so, not for long. The pines are green burnings. The river is another sky, maybe the original. A barred owl calls: *Cackalacka, Cackalacka.* Wrens say what they say and quickly. It is a distinct freedom knowing that my ears are not capable of hearing much more than this. No other life wants me more than any other. The lichen becomes faces. They are solemn and do not glare but look deeply into a side closer than the one I'm breathing the air of. December hunkers harder. Soon frost, sooner stars. I visit the usual places and find them ever unusual. Perhaps water means god in a language closer than the ones we call our own, for now the stones are dressed as trees and it would be ridiculous if they didn't make me swim before climbing them.

I poke a bit through the floodplain downstream of the bridge. The sun is at its zenith and has been for a while. Perhaps the earth's orbit, like the tides, has a period of ebbing. The day is mild. I cannot see any other beings with hearts. There are probably birds, muskrats, and beaver not far away, or even closer, maybe staring at me, maybe inside me, but I don't see them. It's a matter of time.

For instance, the black oak with all the orange voyagers it won't let go of. And the cedar beyond it. Something dehydrated about the sky, a blue like fasting.

The muddy demi-cove is rough with clawmarks. Evidence of other lives. Kingfisher nests in burrows in the banks. Muskrat, raccoon.

The river is gentle. Even where it breaks its last mirrors at the lowhead dam and tries to crawl back up, its very falling is a pleasant tune. Ominous roars do not exist here, not in flood or in drought. It is a river of vowels soft and softly accented.

December gets to the origins, especially the last days of darkening before the slow stretching of light begin. It pares things down. I sense if not the beginning of things, then their foundations. That is enough.

I cannot assert that the beginnings are more present in winter than in summer's densities, but the ground gives certain hints. Those hints, compounded with those in the veins of leaves and spanning of blossoms, the little signals of thunder and ice and rainbows, are enough.

It's out here, on these jaunts, becoming submerged, deeply and lightly, not trying too hard, when I sense there are many worlds. The scum, the wan-undulant water, the sky, and the logs. Yet this is the only world, the never-only, the one ending I can count on never to stop ending or bearing sand and nuts and other surprises. Again the heron—where did it come from?— slaps me against a miracle before swallowing me whole.

Without foliage, the rains goes straight to the river. More origins, more digestion. There are rains. Days of rain.

I haven't seen the river run as it does now. There's a vaguely rubber smell coming from the water. I credit the soil, of which the water bears a good deal. It is a torrent of soil and root tea. Logs drift in and on it, so many plowblades.

The river tills itself. No places are stagnant upstream of the dam now. There goes a log with two orange leaves curled on it. Where the dam is usually visible, a wave has formed thirty to forty feet across, three feet high and glassy save at the edges where foam piles in a curling motion towards the pulsing, breaking center, the peak. It is a crazy brown parenthesis. The middle pounces like many waves within the wave. From edge to edge the wave peels, a conveyor of froth or froth's cousin, which is faith going north instead of east in a different outfit each minute. The sky surfs the wave like so much string cheese.

I keep thinking there will be a bird in the river birch or in the alder, but if there is I don't see it. The trees are up to their ears in water. Logs appear downstream that I missed seeing when they surged through the gauntlet. Maybe they were underwater. I sit on a cement wall that's normally eight feet above the water. The river begins to pulse over the wall's crest, reaching with shallow fingers.

The eddy, a cacophony of moil, water berming in so many strange paisleys. The eddy keeps grabbing new sticks and branches, and then it shuttles them into the wave. It's a gorgeous orbit. There are orbitings within that orbit, little whirlpools at the margin of downstream and upstream flow. There's a waterfall at the place on the cement wall where I sat a few minutes ago.

The plants, the banks, they hold what ground they can hold. Now there are three waterfalls on the cement wall. After the initial swell of the wave, there are two curls below it, smaller and with shallower troughs though equal energy. A wave is not its face so much as its trough, that's the way it goes.

The eddy wants to go home and moves with such force I think it could crawl back to the source. Everything's burst and curl and froth and swirl, but less cute than that because I'm swimming in this opera even as I sit, dry but for my fanny.

The wave is not a tongue any more than it's a bellydance, a field of hyperactive haystacks. Sometimes when a piece of the crest reaches forward, it curls hollow and, breaking, sends a tender mist straight up even as a crowded fingering of foam lurches horizontally upstream. At times, above that pulse, there's a sharp slap, more like a click than a roar.

I wonder how far inland the energy moves. And through what roots and critters. There was something, even while making the bed, unsettling in the air this morning. I don't need proof to blame it on the flood. There go two logs, each at least sixty feet long. They are crossed, the skinnier one on top. A Dr. Pepper bottle floats in the crux of their joinery. They move slowly, but they move.

The bottom of the river must be an exciting place now. Place is commotion. The river is not the same as it is when I begin each breath. Each breath is a river and a log in another river. One could paddle a canoe over the cement wall where I sat ten minutes ago. The bottom is on the surface. How iron, how clay. And bubbles like dirty, shining lace. There is mist, too, of course, whether December is the right word for these days or not.

A week later and the river's still murky from the rains. Beech leaves turn in the currents, the trees on the bank enrattled with gusts. The canoe's bow breaks the chop as I paddle it nowhere in particular, just make it go and keep it from flipping. Cold sun, banks slick and matted where the water has receded. There's an iron quality to the light, a metallic glare. The mountain laurel is blue and at times ghostly so. I hunker against the cold, back sore with work and play. The roots and the trees along the banks, their slender, silt-stained trunks, seem as unsettlingly human as I feel wooden.

The water is not cold. I want it colder. I want it almost ice, a kind of slush. Purity allures. It isn't even dirty out here. Nothing is stained that hasn't belayed its weakest parts down the cliffs of awe and terror of that awe. The wind blows the canoe against the bank where every tree's enspiraled with strangle. Vines twist with such exactitude. There's a two- to three-inch gap at every turn of the vine. I wonder if such a regular dimension is due to the pace of growth. It's odd and somewhat delightful that no matter how fat the tree which hosts the vine, the segments between each turn are close to the same distance. Perhaps it has something to do with grip, how the bark of the vine adheres to that of the tree. As the vines age and thicken, the gap might close, yet at the same time the tree stretches as it grows, so things must even out.

One day I explore a new place. Through the woods there are more woods. Two creeks come together here, each singing through a bottomland of mixed hardwood with an occasional cedar and pine. There's Christmas fern lobey and green among sedge and Japan grass and grape vine. There's polypody and galax and much else. The sun's juice just spills over the horizon; slowly it spreads, shadows spreading with it.

I sit by a fallen pine's upended root wall, a mass of curry-colored soil, stone, root, vines. Birdshit stains two of the roots, white splotches stunning with clarity. It's the coldest day of winter so far, and the woods seem hushed with it. Even the wind in the beech leaves passes with a more delicate rattle.

The woodpeckers begin shallowly and with a rapid drilling. Though seated, I'm tossed and turned in winter's belly. The wind rises for the first time all day, gusty, as if the woods and the sky are having a laugh.

There's ice in the depression made by the absence where roots stood (rootwall) with a tree's falling. Bent, distressed, pale at the edges, it's my favorite kind of ice, little more than a skim coat. The leaves—chestnut and black oak, beech—are visible in their little womb beneath that cold hardness.

There's another pool closer to the hinge where the rootwall stands, and it's unfrozen, even the edges. The root may yet harbor the heat, but most likely it protects the space from cold air and wind. Overhead, two geese are bantering. In the spit between these pools, there are little spires of dirty ice.

Days pass. I come back to the river, sit on a log by the beached canoe. Crows, their sound making the void feel even closer. The day is young, though it already seems to be getting dark, as with some shadowself. Thawsounds abound, a crinkly noise edging from the mud. Fingers of dirty ice topple. The cutbank keeps cutting itself. Bits of dirt come loose and roll, edgy with being frozen.

Last night's hard freeze softens under the slow sun. Light is still on the ice by the river's banks, but it tremors in pulses midstream. There's a deer leg in a tangle of sticks the last flood left. Was a small deer. The river runs with strength, water still soiled and mossy green with last week's rains.

It's like an invisible rain is rising. There is no mist. No leaves fall. Meaning split before there was such a concept. Or spilt. There are as many camps as there are lines—I meant to say lives—in the silted sycamore leaf, and all of them are inhabited by abandon.

How brief a long time feels in winter. There are so many moons on the river now. All of them are not crescent. Some wax, others wane.

As the air warms, new ridges in the ice soften enough to give the light back stronger. It's a map of ancient energies, a particle discourse. Ice was always the origin of flow. I can see the motions, the directions of those motions in the lines, especially as they sweat.

Even in winter there's something crowded and alive about the Piedmont woods. Looking into them, I'm reminded of friends when they're strung out and weary with overwork and overplay and it's clear that no matter how much they try to rest, the only way to clear the malaise is by getting back to the grind. The shaggy river birch, patter of rain, the engorged sky and honeysuckle's green, all of it bleeds together in a cold, raw stock. The world feels like what I find in a bottle left for decades in the duff. It's sinuous and beautiful, yes, beautiful, I know it again and again, and messy, a soreness in the joints and chapped lips. I kiss it with my own bluing, cracked ones.

And here comes the sun to slip me the tongue. Every yesterday was this marvelous, whether I saw it that way or not. One

111

breath, the next, and anyway I'm a little more brightly demolished than I was a year ago. The light reveals the slickness of the
wet trees, the gathered droplets and curves of branches and
trunks. Straight is rare around here. The closest things to
straight—the goldenrod stalk, an oak's trunk where it gets chatty
with the sky, a few cracks in the silt—even those seem bendy and
jointed.

I watch a squirrel's tail quiver as the long animal leaps and
scampers. Such motions seem a way to shake off the rain. Squirrel runs head first down a moss- and vine-licked tree. There are
four bunches of mistletoe in the tree's branches, though they
look more like a mess of tiny, dark green birds perching there.
Winter is a portal. There are woods within the woods.

I cannot speak of insects. The rain is turning to ice. Maybe
it was snow higher up. All I know is what I don't see and do not
say. This will change in a minute ago or an hour. What is certain
is what's behind the bark. I fill my nose and lungs with the damp
air and try to taste the roots.

River oats crackle and rub. Winter grows loud, shrinks
louder. Cold air crisps the leaves that fell and those that hang on.
If moisture remains in their veins, it's hardened with the freeze.
The boulders by creek's edge are membraned with frozen splash-
ings. Water between and over them. The ice is as a colony of
crystal slugs on the stones. Water like white fingers grabs with
the gradient like gravity's hands. Sometimes everything out here
seems a version of gloves: the stones, the driftwood, the sand and
the trees and leaves.

Winter was never austere. My winters in the northcountry
seem in memory as dense and busy as summers in the Piedmont
of the middle south. Even now there are many stalks reaching
just above the river's flow. They're bent with the flow and with
dollops of ice as lensed and blinky as a dragonfly's lookers. They

bounce with the current. They pulse and some of them hold leaves.

Wind is responsible for winter's indulgences. It has so much more room to do its thing. The sky, too, sprawls. The wind is often the sky's way of speaking and listening both. For some things, humans included, speaking is listening; they are the kind I want to hear.

I suspect the river flows differently in such cold. Its load, besides the sediment, is alive, and those organisms probably have a different density as the temperature falls. The water itself on a molecular level might get a little sluggish or else jazzed by the threats and promises of freeze.

The ice inside the ice is the ice. Now a water thrush lands in a maple sapling a few feet away, bobbing its keel and looking around. The pines on the ridge have been swaying a long time and the rhododendron leaves are tightly rolled. What to say of the ferns' nodes except they are homeless too.

January
Like Sky

The listenings are more ample in winter. Barrenness breeds them. They are everywhere in the trees and soil and plants, but they are even more prevalent in the scraggly, wilted edges. The vines sing the melody of larvae feeding under stones that are underwater. Placid licks its chops. The silt on the boulder's low flanks bears the river's finger paintings. I hear a squirrel. I see a log and then a bird where I thought there was a squirrel.

I'm in the canoe. The air is warm. The sky ferments. Maybe it lactates. The sun hides, but I can hear it laughing.

To get to know this place, I'm going to have to leave it. By trying to know it, I am leaving it.

The water dimples through a tangle of sticks near where I drift midstream. The river, where its flow is broken by wood or stone, resembles the clouds. The pattern is slightly washboard, the reflected clouds more orange than they appear in the sky.

Rivers are the clouds of the earth. The trees are the birds. Every rock is a star. I paddle through galaxies near and exploding. Nothing is large, but things are not close either. The beech trees hold their leaves. The beech leaves hold their trees.

Now the sun appears like the sky was opening its eye.

I look up and see the outcrop, a house-sized boulder. I did not expect to come this far. There are winter-dead weeds in the crevices. They seem to be spilling. The whole rock moves by virtue of its electrons.

Each day, the river dives into me. Everywhere does not mean everywhere anymore. There is a pine and looking at it sprinkles my tongue with cayenne. Something surfaces that's a bubble but more accurately breath.

A vulture turns against dark clouds. The land is thick with winter heat, smells of leaf and ground and water that is cooler than air. The big black bird holds, facing south against the breeze. I sit in the canoe. I look at the river, the stones, the sticks hung on the stones. A light drizzle fell overnight, but there hasn't been significant rain in a couple of weeks. The air remains above fifty degrees even in the small of morning.

Many stones are blue. They're long and rectangular, good for staring, sitting on. The vulture is out of sight. My eyes go to a branch-end that tremors midstream. A foot of the branch extends from the water, the rest of it hangs underneath. It appears to shiver. I sit more solidly, watching as though the thin wood is registering the river's pulse, soothing my own. The motion's a steady, frenetic twitching like the tip of a fishing rod against which a fish, alive, tugs and yanks.

May's in the air like food in the teeth. It's not unusual, nor is it confusing. A burst milkweed pod lies within spitting distance. The innards resemble plucked feathers, breast feathers. They're downy with a hard white sheathing at one end. I rub the mass in my fingers and my flesh seems to whisper with the softness. I've been closer to ecstasy but never for so long or warmly.

The river is a book of sparks. Here's one page. Pages are always being torn from the oaks. Though it's morning, the day with its warmth after a night of warmth feels very old. The stones print the music while the words for that music are born in the gaps between thought. The stick tremors still, gives the river's surface a widening mouth. My teeth turn to milkweed. The river has no shadow, but there are ridges where the sky descends for a time.

Now more than twenty bluebirds flit in the depths of a beech tree that leans over the river thick with last summer's leaves. Yes, they're bluebirds. The tree is backlit and the birds' features were not apparent until a few of them flew to the other side of the river, where there's another beech about the same height but with fewer leaves. The bluebird's breast is the same copper of beech leaves. Their noise mirrors their motion. It almost seems that what's audible is their movement more than their throat.

And what of the heron whose slow, labored growl conforms to its flight. The fast chatter of ducks with their quick wingbeats. How the crows bob and flutter both in the throat and in the air.

It has been mild for days. I'm easily distracted and led astray towards some new, terrible wonder. The cool morning fog has lifted. The river continues to drop, exposing new layers of cutbank—the whiskers of roots, clay grottoes, and beds of moss. The holly trees have never seemed so present. There are no holly trees here, only mountain laurel, and they will do.

The woods feel busy with gaps. The more I focus on them, the more full the emptiness feels, especially the sun explaining the ferns' translucent fronds, how the beech leaves' flesh is kin to that of elephants. The body finds the underwater far from water. The body finds what it needs. It needs what it finds. One is never far from water when it comes to the terrain that links thought. The river does not stop in its flow. It may back up, but it finds its way through, over, under, or around in due time.

The sun is not strong enough to burn off the fog. The sky is pale lavender and the beech leaves seem whiter now. There are no flying squirrels, but a tangled piece of fallen branch resembles the one I watched years ago when winter camping in the north woods. The branch appears to be a squirrel in mid-glide, seen from the rear and at a slight angle.

The grey squirrels that are native to these woods are nowhere in sight. The grey stone brings them back. For being such quick, fidgety, sprightly animals, they seem to know, too, the stillnesses of stone.

The woods never lack activity, but they are rarely more subtle in their motions than at winter's heart. The myriad forms and their equally far-ranging colors, smells, textures, motions, are no revelation. There are constant surprises. They constantly play with me. When I sit long enough, I'm surprised by what is in front and around me. I could sit forever and a certain bend of leaf, its mold or its veins, would throw me in wonder's time capsule.

These woods have been here for a long time, yet they are changing and staying the same with all the regularity and mystery as the sky and the sun that drives their being. It is a melting pot of landscape, the Piedmont, a place through which by water the mountains meet the coast. It was once mountains and it was once coast and now there is a squirrel, I don't know where it came from, but it's a ruckus in the leaves. Is it feeding, messing around? Is it bearing the voices I once tried so hard to escape by coming here, by looking at squirrels? There are three beech trees near it, each with many leaves, each tree's leaves a different shade of brown. The tree with the darkest leaves is not the smallest. They grow on a slope that faces east.

I can't see or hear the squirrel anymore. It hasn't moved. It isn't gone. It is somewhere else.

More often, this winter, I walk. It has to do with time. And curiosity, its legs and arms, paddles and hulls, breathing and drifting. One lunchbreak I walk where the prior day the river ran. My feet slide in the soft mud left by receding water. There are coon tracks, impressions of toes rich with detail. It seems that the raccoon stepped carefully, was in no hurry.

There are new logs on the banks. There are old logs in new positions. Everything is soggy. Flood-abandoned leaves tangle the laurel bushes. The laurel tangles my way.

There is no untangling of the Piedmont woods. A tree has fallen recently, as if the river clipped it. It might have been rotten. Where the runoff moved down the slopes, there are gouged paths in the leaves, banks of clumped sogginess as well as bare places of exposed soil.

Even now leaves as they dry roll the slopes. The wind is brisk, but it feels thin. It's not a nourishing wind. The rain has ushered a cold front. I probably won't see another string of mild days for some time.

Weather is simple. It changes. I say the clouds are grey and the wind is thin, but the clouds are as purple as an iris and the wind could house a nation. There is no wind now. The limbs shiver yet. The only tense of weather is past perfect. There is no here and now except the now where then is here and soon is here.

Only water lives in the present. Downstream is upstream and the mouth is the source. Time evaporates even as it nourishes the gilled ones. I turn at a tributary and leave the river. I no longer worry the being here. I bring the voices with me that I once tried so hard to escape. I hold the voices close to my heart where they sometimes bloom, sending gentleness from petals down to the roots. Soon there are small cliffs and a stream breaking down rock faces. The bark is swollen and the moss damp. There are pools where the trickling is in stereo. Landscape's secrets are its gifts. Much is buried and more has gone to rot or washed downstream. Every rise is a bottomland too.

The water is clear in the small stream along which I now stand and sometimes step. It is shallow, but the depth is more visible than in the river that runs clouded and thick with mud. I poke around. I duck through a stand of laurel, scale a boulder, mount a steppe. The more I look, the more I am entangled. The sphagnum resembles millipedes and ferns. The horizon foams at the mouth. The Piedmont is the easiest landscape I've ever known. It is the least simple, however. Its only threat its lack of threat. The sky shuffles its deck, readies a new trick.

The limbs grow foliage as they lie reflected on the breeze-rippled water. I sense it being far too cold for foliage or growth, and move forward by being wrong. Perception is always accurate, even when it is wrong. The sun shrinks to an oval as it squeezes between the pines. Raw, cold air liberates. I'm another crack in the world's lips, let it bleed.

It's no longer difficult for me to call a place sacred. Forever I've believed, without knowing it, in the sacred, but mostly I spelled it scared. If now and then I feel a sacred energy, it involves a response to everything I fear and love, though I'm not aware of that then, in that moment. The cold is greedy even as it's spare, allows room to roam. The eyes see further while the body feels less and much more tingly. Back at the river and I have no word for the way the leaves hang matted and clustered from the vines. The flood left them that way. Flood might be the only word.

The birds are very quiet in their presence. I hear their cheets and chorts as though underwater and they just above the surface. When the body is cold, the mind works slower and more efficiently too.

The earth has turned so the sun is dilated again. The pines are where they always are and won't stay. A gnat drifts on the shine, its wings in motion holding the light like a minute cloud. The cold teases every next breath with a trusting abandon.

I am slowly ecstatic. Even in warm weather, rapture takes its time with me. The vines seem to emigrate. Because the world is sacred, there's room for rapture. Always the ferns shrink with the cold. When the air grows warm, will the ferns assume their prior size? The sand and silt linger a bluer brown. On days like this—everything green no longer green, ice at the edges, the ink hardening—the sycamores run the place. Their legs may be asleep, but look at the bark. Gracious, the mistletoe in the hickory is a shambles. I'm not talking about a neck of the woods, but the woods' feet and fingers, its ribcage and seething organs.

Another day. Snow falls. Ice hangs from the rocks like lichen drool. The flakes stick to the rocks and leaves and trees and ground. I see things that I might not see in sun or clouds or rain: the texture of stones, how the flakes stay on the flatter, more horizontal places and in the sinuous grooves, but not in other spots because they're too steep or wet. It's the same way with the trees and even the leaves and limbs. Tufts of snow gather at the crux of limb and trunk and in the nubs of old limbs, the burls and grooves of bark. Technically, they call such snow a dusting, but it falls steady so who knows what will happen.

The big flakes are numerous and seem with their size to fall slowly, so many commas on the sentences of air. Snow makes me earnest. It loves me slow, ignores me slower. I enter a pace like falling. My heart beats differently. I walk. There is nobody, no footprints of human or other animal. The crowded woods along this river can be places of exquisite privacy, despite its proximity to busy highways, cities, and towns. It's hard to find this kind of intimacy in well known, more dramatic places, the ones on the covers of the glossies; I've tried.

I return to the gulch. The gulch always rewards my visits with a surprise or two. I always leave it both more and less sure of the woods. Today a beech tree stuns me with its forked trunk. It resembles certain sycamore trees along the creek one watershed from here. It resembles cypress trunks, too. It appears as though the tree has grown two arms that reach one to the boulder and one to the ground for added stability.

I look from the beech to the icicles on a moss-emerald seepage cliff, the shriveled yet deep green polypody. Something swarms in my belly, a nest of bees, a blizzard, the flakes light and the accumulation deep and honeyed.

The icicles are wet. It isn't cold enough for them to tinkle and glimmer with the dry hard shine of ice in extreme cold. Now one falls with a sequence of high pitched tinkling along the cliff behind which I sit under an outcrop. Another falls, then another. It sounds like the recycling being emptied. There are traffic-sounds in the distance and water running over rocks and leaves on the rocks in the nearground.

Small, rounded lumps of ice grow at the base of the seepage cliffs, a gentler version of the more spiked and pointed ice above them. Maybe, if such weather continues, the two units of ice will grow together, making one.

There's a bubble on a rock down which water slides. The bubble hangs from a leaf matted to a place more level than the steep-lying stone. The membrane of liquid quivers as other bubbles traveling down with the water bounce and slide from it. It's okay to hold the world this way, lightly, letting what comes touch me and move on.

The bubble pops. The smaller, more rattley, sleet-like precipitation might have punctured it. I don't know. I don't even know where I'm going. There is something the woods will show me, whether they mean to or not.

These days, even when I'm not in the woods, I'm in the woods. And I love it when the wind hurls bits of slush from the limbs, when the slush splashes on the leaves, is sliced by pine needles. I'm in the woods, and I won't stay long. I never stay long. I stay forever. The sky is bruise and the air lukecold. A glaze that won't harden covers the land.

A messy, delightful scene. The heavy and damp air makes a kind of womb. I sit at the edge of land that was clearcut not ten years ago. Foresters seeded it with loblollies which hang in all manner of bend, luscious with the weight of half-hardened water. A hawk flies over the tract's far edge. It's more than a grove. The green mass of young pines extends many acres downridge to a drainage feeding the creek.

From a place on a rise, the trees appear as a green pond. When I walk through it, it's a kind of swimming, a cold dip. I wonder what sort of animals inhabit the place. The hawk must be attracted to something, fieldmouse, songbird. The place resembles a pond because there's a distinct border where the pines end and the winter-bare hardwoods begin. The needled density, thick with mixed precipitation, creates a different sense of depth than that of the hardwood forest. There's more breathing room for the lungs and eyes among the lower reaches of oaks and maple, beech and laurel.

It's not the barrenness of the clearcut, but its density that impresses me. There's nothing close to dormant about these woods. The plants, weather, sky, and critters are always scrambling, it seems, to fill in the gaps by making more gaps.

Like the sky is a not too young child that has recently learned to spit and may have an obsessive quality about it. Lord knows my boots are wet.

Accuracy is not everything, but it's close. I don't come to the woods to be an expert at anything. I come here to see where I'll be led and let myself be lost enough to be led.

My destination is wandering, my motive not clarity but surprise. Emptiness means acceptance that the void is full of everything and nothing, more crowded than God's voicemail.

I walk differently. I walk the same.

The ground is slippery and makes walking a discovery of muscles in my legs and hips between which vocal, feathered things fly and perch. The Piedmont does not reward experts, no place does. Anyway landscape is always an event, a play that never stops running. I try to catch a scene by entering it. Maybe love will join me. Probably love is already waiting.

I grab the trees as I slip the steeper slopes, and they sprinkle me with hardened lenses. I would like to know more about the crows. I'm probably closer to crows when I'm elbow deep in being afraid, maybe, or doing the dishes, taking my time with them.

There's a mountain laurel, a young one. Many of its leaves are torn. Various shapes and shades of green, variations on oval. I can see how the flesh holds waves formerly known as purple, especially when I look through the blobs of frozen water. Not one leaf is bare of root-colored mottlings, little Rorschach bull's-eyes where the pigment has changed.

The woods are metamorphic. I don't walk, I crunch. There's another mantle now. The light is broken to new wholes and halved more than twice. The river looks burnt, the ashes and coals of all the diamond fires in the trees. My feet are tongues on a giant rock candy. Cold is a kind of teething. There's no time for liquid unless it is deep enough to generate its own heat. The freeze is general in a hard, specific way. I'm also shrink-wrapped, my fingers especially.

What has happened to the slush is a model of what happened to the ground that it exists as it does now. The pines have a new, temporary skin, but it's a shell, a plastron. Awareness was always promiscuous.

And now I'm walking around the pond. Two otters are playing, yes, playing. One keeps popping through the ice. There are twenty holes at least.

It's good to be back at the pond. I look for the grebe that visited last winter. There are geese and otters visible. There are signs of beaver and cold weather.

Bluebirds flash along the perimeters of the fields at the pond's southeast edge. Edgeplaces delight me with the depth, their intermingling of light and shadow and life. Breath is less breath than a saying thank you for such being. Wind is chapped air. My lips have not for long been so smooched. How the sun-tongues do lick, cold with beginnings. The icy, wintry mix feels more indigenous than the pines. Complaint has no room to breathe among such shining. The shadows grow legs and burrow at the ellipses of their becomings. I am not empty. The emptiness fills me with the rhythms of all promise. I cannot see the end of existence. There's no warmer bed than simply walking. Look at the ferns, the dead Japan grass's milky saffron glow. Elsewhere could not be any closer than now.

I walk the pond and another pond awakens in me. I see the land before there was a pond, the former forests, the former seas and sediments. In the Precambrian the Piedmont was underwater, all possibility. The air is alive with creation. One breath, the next, and I sing the motions of the otters' emergences and divings. I sense them inside me no more than I sense myself inside them. One otter bursts through the ice just as the wind accelerates. We have a brief stare. The illusion of the world before me glows with the illusion of the inner world, and the two illusions make it real. There are no beginnings. Everything is beginning, who cares how long it's been going at it. The otter dives. I still stare. The hole begins to freeze. The ice's drift. I am singed with cold. I sing.

A few days cold and then deeply mild. I'm back at the river. The water bulges in its course through a run of small boulders and cobble. The air smells like thaw. Bright sun scrapes its nails along every wave. I can't look for long. It's good to be warm in a t-shirt. There are great mats of flooddrift at varying intervals along the bank. I scan them for treasures, wood in pleasing shapes and with a polish soft as cool flesh. I find a doll's head, plastic with silt-matted hair and a face on either side, one awake and one sleeping. I hold it and see for a moment out the back of my head. The view is nearly the same, a holly tree instead of ironwood, more woods instead of river.

It could be the temperature or the lengthening days. Last night the moon was full and I loaded my canoe as though to paddle it. When I paddle a river in moonlight, I don't paddle a river, I paddle the moon. I don't even paddle, or if I do, I don't know it. Space claims me. I sense more fully my kinship to dust.

Some relative of moonlight abides in the pourover waves and the curtains of flume on the downstream edge of barely submerged stones. There's a promise of salamanders in this light. And now the air is both the taste of warm butter and the texture of cold butter on the tongue. Thaw is a kind of cream. I want to say honey, as I do, but I cannot. Winter's pollen is more grey than gold. I say beeswax. I say flame, not of burning but the image emblazoned on the eye the moment I've blown the fire out.

I sit on a log. The bark resembles scales, seems overly dry, curls and clings like tired shingles on a house long condemned. Out here nothing is condemned, not even a lack of rapture. The beaver know I am here. They know that I abandoned hope a long time ago, that I am emptying, diminishing into another realm, another seasoning. Is zings, zing a kind of tryst, turtling. They know, the beaver.

The river is a roof also, of slate. Beneath it is an atmosphere or just more being, and beneath that is the bottom, which is always, no matter how far down I travel, a roof. The only ladder is that of the body loving what it will as well as it may.

The holly leaves are motionless on the wind-swaying branches. Their stems and their flesh are too rigid for bending. The green river appears as a motion picture of the holly leaves' essence. Flared with every wave, and the water turning white along the peaks and ridges of the textures, is as spires. I'm pricked through and through. A surface is never less than depth.

One day near the end of January, I sit on a boulder that's a grove of moss and polypody and silt and a few shrubs and small trees. I'm near the river. There is ice on the banks. From a distance the ice appears as wads of soggy tissue partly submerged, a lavender tint to that smudge.

What is a grove? The body is a grove and a body in the woods is a grove on the move. But can any two plants existing in certain niche of a landform, as responsible for the landform as the land and weather, erosion processes and such, can a small system like that be a grove?

I know that the ice, the more I watch it, warms me. I know that reckoning involves muscles, and that memory is body as much as presence is. I know, too, that the fat and water and blood and sinews and bones of reckoning define a place as a sum of groves, of loves and growths.

I am this place (don't say it). The sycamore tree with white trunks and limbs, a white brighter now than any cloud—and there are clouds—the sycamore makes the oaks and other brown-barked hardwoods seem redundant, endless with shadows and angles and an endless variation among them.

I breathe heavier now. There are roots in my lungs. My breath smells like the stuff that clings to my boots after some wading. I taste the smell. I taste the muck. Between being and thought is a grove, and I tangle there even as the sparrows drag me as if an aphid into the warmth. The canopy is a maze of capillaries. Slowly the gaps between thought stretch out. The only language I breathe is that which the land offers. It tastes like sky.

Acknowledgments

Much sweetgum to the editors of the following publications in whose pages many of these chapters first appeared, sometimes in slightly different form: *About Place*, *atLength*, and *Taproot*.

And sweetgum, sweetgum, and more sweetgum for my friends and family, as well as my colleagues and students at UNC-Chapel Hill and Hollins University.